Beyond Free College

About The Futures Series on Community Colleges

The Futures Series on Community Colleges is designed to produce books that will shape the future of community colleges by examining emerging structures, systems and business models, and stretching assumptions about leadership and management by reaching beyond the limits of convention and tradition.

Richard L. Alfred, Series Founding Editor, Emeritus Professor of Higher Education, University of Michigan

Debbie L. Sydow, Series Senior Editor, President, Richard Bland College of the College of William and Mary

Kate Thirolf, Series Editor, Dean of Business & Human Services, Jackson College

Books in The Futures Series on Community Colleges

Reinventing the Community College Business Model: Designing Colleges for Organizational Success by Christopher Shults

Community Colleges as Economic Engines by Kjell A. Christophersen

Artificial Intelligence, Mixed Reality, and the Redefinition of the Classroom by Scott M. Martin, Contributions by Christopher Jennings

Competing on Culture: Driving Change in Community Colleges by Randall VanWagoner

The Completion Agenda in Community Colleges: What It Is, Why It Matters, and Where It's Going by Chris Baldwin

Financing Community Colleges: Where We Are, Where We're Going By Richard Romano and James Palmer

Unrelenting Change, Innovation, and Risk: Forging the Next Generation of Community Colleges by Daniel J. Phelan

The Urgency of Now: Equity and Excellence by Marcus M. Kolb, Samuel D. Cargile, et al.

Developing Tomorrow's Leaders: Context, Challenges, and Capabilities by Pamela Eddy, Debbie L. Sydow, Richard L. Alfred, and Regina L. Garza Mitchell

Community Colleges on the Horizon: Challenge, Choice, or Abundance by Richard Alfred, Christopher Shults, Ozan Jaquette, and Shelley Strickland

Re-visioning Community Colleges by Debbie Sydow and Richard Alfred

Community College Student Success: From Boardrooms to Classrooms by Banessa Smith Morest

First in the World: Community Colleges and America's Future by J. Noah Brown

Minding the Dream: The Process and Practice of the American Community College, Second Edition by Gail O. Mellow and Cynthia M. Heelan

Beyond Free College

Making Higher Education Work for 21st-Century Students

Eileen L. Strempel and Stephen J. Handel

Series Founding Editor: Richard L. Alfred
Series Senior Editor: Debbie L. Sydow
Series Editor: Kate Thirolf

ROWMAN & LITTLEFIELD
Lanham • Boulder • New York • London

Published by Rowman & Littlefield
An imprint of The Rowman & Littlefield Publishing Group, Inc.
4501 Forbes Boulevard, Suite 200, Lanham, Maryland 20706
www.rowman.com

6 Tinworth Street, London, SE11 5AL, United Kingdom

British Library Cataloguing in Publication Information Available

Library of Congress Cataloging-in-Publication Data

Names: Strempel, Eileen, author. | Handel, Stephen J., 1958– author.
Title: Beyond free college : making higher education work for 21st-century students /
  Eileen L. Strempel and Stephen J. Handel.
Description: Lanham : Rowman & Littlefield, [2021] | Series: The futures series on
  community colleges | Includes bibliographical references and index. | Summary:
  "Beyond Free College seeks greater investment in higher education by promoting
  a single metric-lower-cost-per-degree-granted-as the driver of a transfer pathway.
  The book aims to spur higher education advocates to reorganize the transfer function
  to serve neotraditional students in ways that advance completion, not just access to
  higher education"— Provided by publisher.
Identifiers: LCCN 2020042184 (print) | LCCN 2020042185 (ebook) | ISBN
  9781475848649 (cloth) | ISBN 9781475848656 (paperback) | ISBN 9781475848663
  (ebook)
Subjects: LCSH: Students, Transfer of—United States. | College credits—United
  States. | College costs—United States. | Educational mobility—United States. |
  Community colleges—United States. | Nontraditional college students—United
  States. | Educational equalization—United States. | Education, Higher—Aims and
  objectives—United States.
Classification: LCC LB2360 .S86 2021 (print) | LCC LB2360 (ebook) | DDC
  371.2/9140973—dc23
LC record available at https://lccn.loc.gov/2020042184
LC ebook record available at https://lccn.loc.gov/2020042185

♾️™ The paper used in this publication meets the minimum requirements of American
National Standard for Information Sciences—Permanence of Paper for Printed Library
Materials, ANSI/NISO Z39.48-1992.

"Citizenship in the United States has never come with a guaranteed standard of living or political influence. Historically, however, it has offered the possibility of upward mobility. And it has provided means for citizens to improve their understanding of public life and their capacity to participate in it, thereby enhancing democracy. Not many decades ago, higher education was an important key to this dynamic."

—Suzanne Mettler, *Degrees of Inequality:*
How the Politics of Higher Education
Sabotaged the American Dream
(New York, NY: Basic Books, 2014), p. 18.

Contents

Preface

"Over half of all students on a typical campus at any given point in time, on average, are mobile students: They either came from somewhere else, will go somewhere else, or both, before finishing a degree."

—Douglas Shapiro, "Student
Transfer and Mobility"[1]

When we began to write this book, we were focused on the traditional transfer function between America's community colleges and four-year institutions—an academic pathway that allowed students attending a community college to prepare themselves for transfer to a four-year college (usually at the start of their junior year) so that they could earn a baccalaureate degree. As long-term champions of transfer, we viewed this unique pathway as one of the most transformative innovations in higher education.

In what other sphere of US higher education can an individual lacking formal education credentials, a privileged background, or financial resources enter college possessing merely ambition and drive? And in what other postsecondary education institution other than a community college would this individual be authentically welcomed as the center of the institution's mission and provided with access to education and training that is low cost, geographically convenient, and aligned with the intellectual aims of four-year institutions?

Equally impressive are four-year institutions—mostly public, but some prominent private ones as well—who admit large numbers of community college students as if they were first-year entrants; this is an authentic educational partnership often unheralded by critics who only see higher education institutions as isolated bastions of irrelevance and bloat.

Now over a hundred years old, the transfer function legacy in America is unique. Nevertheless, transfer seems almost unthinkable, especially when compared to traditional perspectives of college-going in the United States that emphasize carefully manicured lawns, Greek revival architecture, and eighteen-year-old students moving into high-rise dormitories, complete with climbing walls, swimming pools, and meditation pods. That such clichés are seen as sufficient descriptors of higher education in America is belied by a community college system that enrolls 43% of all undergraduates in the nation.[2]

Embedded in a populist educational legacy, community colleges and their sometimes silent but essential four-year institutional partners have established an almost unassailable idea that any individual, possessing requisite motivation and effort, can earn a degree previously granted to only a small proportion of the population. It is this *access* to a previously privileged academic citadel that sustains the energy around the transfer function.

As we embarked on our research, however, we quickly realized that, as remarkable as the transfer function's first century has been, the new millennium brings different challenges. Although we identify these "new challenges" throughout the book, we were surprised, then humbled, by the historical similarities between what nineteenth-century educational visionaries were trying to achieve and the goals of today's innovators.

We were surprised because we thought today's issues in postsecondary education were the result of a stunning and unique transformation in Internet technologies and crushing economic disparities. We were then humbled when we realized that progressive ideals such as calibrating the US education system toward greater access, especially for individuals who might not have access to postsecondary opportunities, was as essential now as it was in the Gilded Age.

Today's higher education concerns are no less urgent than those present a century ago. During the time of the book's gestation, we perceived enormous shifts in the public's view of US higher education, none that were cosmetic or even new, but all gathering momentum collectively in ways unforeseen by even the most adept and savvy of education leaders.

These shifts included steady, seemingly inexorable tuition increases; significant student load debt; stagnant or declining state support for postsecondary education; crushing competition for admission at the most elite universities in the nation; and, finally, a kind of postsecondary moral reckoning in an incident that has come to be referred to as "Varsity Blues."

The notion that animated us most significantly—an ideal most revolutionary to our staid concept of transfer—was the various "free college" proposals advanced by presidential candidates and college and university leaders alike. For us, "free college," regardless of any given proposal's details, ceased to be a radically progressive notion, and became more of a daily, inspirational call rooted in US history.

At the conclusion of WWII, the United States invested heavily in higher education through what came to be known as the G.I. Bill. This investment covered not only the tuition of returning service men and women—the Greatest Generation—but also other significant costs, including fees, books, housing, and food. But the G.I. Bill turned out to be something so much more, as described by political scientist Suzanne Mettler in "Soldiers to Citizens: The G.I. Bill and the Making of the Greatest Generation":

> In an era when advanced education seemed out of reach for most Americans, the G.I. Bill's education and training provisions made it accessible, and did so through broadly inclusive eligibility features and implementation that treated recipients with dignity and respect, as rights-bearing beneficiaries.[3]

Throughout this book, we take as a starting point the transformative quality of national public policy, such as the G.I. Bill, when rightly-envisioned and well-implemented. Thus, our enthusiasm about the free college debate—by no means a public discussion that lacks vigorous and compelling critics—nevertheless echoes a time and place in which our nation viewed higher education policy as part of the fabric and defense of the nation.

After years of neglect, higher education is on the political agenda again. This is because higher education is seen by most American families as the most obvious—if not the best—avenue of economic advancement for their sons and daughters.

With widening income disparities in the United States, the reach of a higher education degree appears increasingly elusive. Furthermore, the seminal *Atlantic* article, "Making the Case for Reparations," calls on America to atone for the legacy of enslavement in our country, and higher education shines as a potential avenue for reckoning with our national debts.[4]

As a result, the role of transfer will be more important than ever in providing entrée to higher education to individuals from populations that have been underserved by more costly, elite institutions. State and federal support of higher education is on unstable ground, even as lawmakers hail the economy-boosting elements of a college-educated populace.

Community colleges remain the least well-funded segment of higher education and yet must accommodate the needs of the most academically challenged students. Meanwhile, corporations such as Starbucks and Google are building their own educational programming and credentials, raising fundamental questions about the nature and value of academic credit. Various mega-universities have emerged, but the outcomes for today's students are highly varied (and, frequently, not as good as one might hope).

Given this confluence of circumstances, public higher education must either cede its postsecondary leadership to industry and partisan oversight or double-down on its transformative legacy. We argue that the latter is the only reasonable strategy, but that such an approach must embrace what we define as the "neo-traditional" student in a broader reconceptualization of transfer ethos.

THE RISE OF THE NEOTRADITIONAL STUDENT

When we think of transfer, the immediate image is of community college students seeking to transfer to a four-year institution to earn a baccalaureate degree. However, this traditional transfer pathway is only one element of an increasingly mobile college-going populace.

Today, transfer is characterized by a variety of academic trajectories as students enroll in multiple postsecondary-education institutions in their pursuit of credentials and degrees. Indeed, the idea that most students today remain at a single institution represents a minority of undergraduates, as noted above by Shapiro's quote.

Transfer is emerging as a critical organizing framework. It serves as the connective tissue linking higher education credit earned in high school, whether from Advanced Placement (AP), International Baccalaureate (IB), dual-enrollment programs, or early college programs, with a host of newer credit models, such as prior-learning assessments (PLA), and new forms of delivery, including competency-based education (CBE), online learning, and the emerging blend of higher education and corporate America with industry-delivered credentials.

Although the core values of successful transfer from a two-year to a four-year institution continue to resonate with those who view higher education as a progressive—rather than an elite—social good, these newer forms of academic credit and delivery are reshaping and reforming the very mission and vision of transfer. For example, students have had the opportunity to accumulate college credit in high school for the past fifty years or so, but today many state legislatures have mandated the use of these programs to speed college completion rates.

These mandates have dramatically increased the number of students enrolling in dual enrollment (DE) and similar programs, but with scant reliance on research to inform the extent to which such choices have met the goal of helping students, especially those from traditionally underrepresented groups, to prepare for and succeed in postsecondary-education institutions. With this book, we set out to understand what really works, and what does not.

In addition to an increased prevalence of "early college" courses in high schools, there is a proliferation of new postsecondary choices, such as online courses, stackable credentials, competency-related learning, and PLA. It is not clear, however, that more choice brings higher postsecondary-education success rates.

A typical transfer student now completes the baccalaureate degree by piecing together credits from four or more sources: AP credit; dual enrollment and various online or competency-based credits; and coursework completed both at the two-year and four-year institution(s). These circuitous pathways, then, provide educational access in a bewildering swirl of credits that challenge institutions and individuals who grapple with how to package them into a culminating degree.

These emerging trends complicate the transfer landscape—a landscape that was already difficult enough to navigate by students who were interested in "traditional" transfer pathways. Could it be true that the new "democratization of education" will simply exacerbate the deepening cultural and economic divisions in America?

Perhaps students from high-income backgrounds will continue to venture on a straight and clear pathway to Harvard and other elite institutions, whereas low-income students will be "encouraged" to take online courses at community colleges or complete prior-learning assessments for transfer credit in the hope that courses will successfully stack into badges, certificates, and, eventually, a degree.

Our view is more optimistic. There has never been a more vital moment for a reimagining of the populist transfer ethos, but one that embraces a profoundly different higher education landscape now and in the future. There seems little argument that national prosperity demands a more educated populace.

But how will this be accomplished in an America increasingly fragmented economically, politically, and culturally? Our singular conceit—that the United States should deepen its investment in higher education—led us to investigate how best this could be accomplished.

As we began to research and write, our limited conception of "transfer" took on new meaning for the twenty-first century. It is our belief that the transfer process of today and tomorrow will serve as the active and central force that fosters student success by tying together the increased number of strands of educational possibility.

This book explores these various educational strands as related to the transfer function and their increasing impact on higher education in America. It then explores how a modern ideation of transfer—while honoring a time when the nation rallied around transformative education policies like the G.I. Bill—might best capitalize on the boldest and best components, bringing the potential of higher education to all of those willing to work for it.

We find ourselves thrillingly inspired by our nation's willingness to invest in "free college," but such initiatives alone may not be the most effective use of public funds if our first priority is boosting college completion rates for students from all economic backgrounds. Instead, we provide research-informed exemplars as alternatives.

Although we honor the historical legacy of the transfer pathway that was developed over a century ago, we are excited that its evolution since that time is poised—as we document in this book—to advance a new generation of Americans toward postsecondary successes that might not otherwise be available to them.

List of Abbreviations

ACE	American Council on Education
ACT	a standardized test used for college admissions in the United States
AI	artificial intelligence
AP	Advanced Placement
APIP	AP Incentive Program
APUS	American Public University System
CAEL	Council for Adult and Experiential Learning
CBE	competency-based education
C-BEN	Competency-Based Education Network
CLEP	College Level Examination Program
CREDIT	College Credit Recommendation Service
DE	dual enrollment
ECHS	early college high school
ETS	Education Testing Service
IB	International Baccalaureate
IPEDS	Integrated Postsecondary Education Date System
PLA	prior-learning assessments
PLTL	peer-led team learning
SAT	a standardized test used for college admissions in the United States

Acknowledgments

Many people helped us to sustain the energy needed to complete this book. Both of us serve on the Advisory Board for the National Institute for the Study of Transfer Students (NISTS) and have benefited from the passionate advocacy and deep knowledge of the members of that organization. Moreover, just as we completed the editing of our second book for NISTS, President Debbie Sydow, the visionary editor for this book series, approached us about refining our transfer experiences for publication. We are enormously thankful for her support and confidence in this project. Special thanks are extended to the University of California, Los Angeles, which provided research support during crucial, later stages of this project; and to the College Board, which encouraged the second author to pursue this and other independent writing projects. Of course neither institution is responsible for the book's content, nor does it necessarily represent the official positions of the University of California or of the College Board or its member institutions. We are also deeply appreciative of the gifted editorial guidance provided by Julia Zafferano, whose professional expertise, as well as gentle chiding, improved our effort considerably, although we are quick to add that all remaining editorial errors are self-inflicted.

Finally, working together on this book has been a tremendous amount of fun. Our weekly accountability conversations kept two busy people motivated, intellectually engaged, actively writing (some weeks more than others), and, best of all, always laughing. Having a co-author, in this particular happy instance, lessened the burden and doubled the joy. In this effort, we were supported daily by family and friends. In particular, Eileen thanks her sons, Gavin and Dylan, with the hope that life-long learning will always capture their hearts in their own postsecondary journeys.

Chapter 1

Transfer Contradictions

Bridging the Academic Divide

"One of the greatest achievements of American higher education, an achievement uniquely ours, is its continued drive—not without conflict and contradiction—toward wider and wider inclusion. . . . What has become increasingly clear over the past few decades, however, is that access is a necessary but not sufficient condition for achieving a robust and democratic system of higher education. It is not enough to let people in the door; we have to create conditions for them to thrive once inside."

—Mike Rose, *Back to School: Why Everyone Deserves a Second Chance at Education*[1]

Contradictions are at the heart of the traditional transfer pathway. These contradictions—in mission, policies, and practices—serve to undermine our confidence in a structure that should otherwise stand as an innovative strategy to expand higher education access. Although the transfer pathway continues to operate despite these contradictions, the growing need for a citizenry with postsecondary credentials compels us to address these contradictions explicitly, working toward greater coherence about our aims in service to student needs.

It is not news to any transfer pathway advocate that this educational pipeline, from the very beginning, represents an artificial structure designed to knit together two- and four-year colleges in a fashion that neither type of institution wholeheartedly supports. Although the aims of both community colleges and four-year institutions overlap in fundamental ways, they also diverge significantly.

1

Despite the potential of the transfer pathway to enhance students' access to higher education, the scratchy relationship between the two postsecondary segments has been steeped in self-interest and a "them vs. us" stance over enrollments, funding, and prestige. It belies the public grandstanding of two- and four-year leaders who often make a confident display of demonstrating their support for transfer and the students who traverse this chasm but who are rarely seen in public with one another.

The different historical, formalistic, and even intellectual worldviews of two- and four-year institutions prepare the groundwork for a set of inherent contradictions that would seem to make them mismatched partners. These contradictions impede the development of authentic transfer pathways, supporting the maintenance of institutional separatism that does not serve transfer students well.

Higher education leaders often identify as strengths the great diffusion and variation of America's colleges and universities, but we wonder if it is a characterization that hides as much it illustrates, diverting us from asking the hard questions about the completion rates of colleges and universities of all stripes. Taken at face value, the profusion of two- and four-year colleges and universities in the United States—private and public, and not-for-profit and for-profit—rarely serves the needs of students who wish to make the jump from one institution to another. These sharp differences among institutions need to be made explicit if we are going to get much traction in advancing the cause of transfer.

In this chapter, we explore the contradictory character of the two-year to four-year traditional institutional transfer pathway along several dimensions: origins and history; missions and motives; populism and elitism; credit and credibility; and revenues and resources.

Each section highlights two- and four-year college worldviews that are institutionally consistent but fundamentally unaligned across institutions. This is not to say that these institutions do not possess a great deal in common; it is where they diverge that most affects students who are caught in the netherworld between them.

ORIGINS AND HISTORY

Community colleges and four-year institutions possess different academic cultures. Although both types of institutions deliver postsecondary education, they sprang from different origins, attract different kinds of students, place different responsibilities on faculty, receive funding from different sources, offer different kinds of curricula, maintain different kinds of physical plants, and are governed by different political processes.

Some will argue that these are merely cosmetic contrasts, an obvious reflection of the diversity of higher education institutions in the United States. One might reasonably claim, in fact, that such differences occur within the universe of community colleges and four-year institutions and, therefore, simply reflect institutional differences, not broader contrasts among educational segments. We argue, however, that these differences serve as the basis for fundamentally different educational worldviews.

These cultural contradictions are embedded in the very creation of community colleges—which, a hundred years ago, were the newest entry into the US postsecondary institutional ecosystem and, at the time, the most radical. Manuel Gomez from the University of California summarizes these contradictions well:

> Community colleges inhabit an essential yet problematic position in American higher education. Essential because they ensure equal educational access, offer students an academic "second chance," and provide vocational and community education in a collegiate environment. The problems, of course, stem from the same components of their very purpose.[2]

Kevin Dougherty, in his classic book *The Contradictory College*,[3] articulates a similar claim, though he is mindful to include four-year institutions as fundamental players in a relationship with two-year institutions that is inherently contradictory:

> As long as community colleges remain two-year institutions, their baccalaureate aspirants will have to overcome the psychological difficulty that, to pursue their degree, they will have to transfer to a new and foreign institution. Even if the university is in the same city, it remains a separate institution, with its own culture and organizational routines. . . . As a result, many students will still choose not to brave the chasm between the institutions.[4]

Steven Brint and Jerome Karabel, in their celebrated book *The Diverted Dream*, go a step further, naming selective four-year institutions as complicit in the establishment of a transfer process that, from the beginning, was designed as a gatekeeper to elite postsecondary education for only the most capable, rather than the democratizing force for which it is often described.[5]

Although it is generally agreed that the origin of community colleges can be traced at least partially to the efforts of leaders of prestigious US universities in the late nineteenth century, their motives were decidedly mixed (we discuss this issue in greater depth in chapter 2). Their desire to fashion what was known then as a "junior college" certainly had populist leanings. Like others, these education leaders saw that a burgeoning US population would need (and want) access to more education to sustain a growing economy.

A concurrent motivation was more self-serving, however. The initiative of a junior college system, which would provide students with courses in the lower-division, was also designed to shield their institutions from an onslaught of new students they could not or did not want to accommodate at the baccalaureate level.

Although the intention never came to pass to have junior colleges deliver the first two years of a collegiate education exclusively (while the elite institutions would focus on the upper division and graduate education), these leaders still viewed two-year colleges as a necessary bulwark against the admissions selectivity they sought to protect. And, in the latter sense, the originators of the community college model succeeded.

The open-access mission of these two-year institutions provides access to almost any individual with a desire to attend college, leaving four-year institutions with the option of choosing the students they admit. It is a kind of institutionally arranged marriage in which the participants, however dedicated and earnest, are nonetheless complicit in a process that serves only some of the students some of the time.

Over three decades ago, researchers Richard C. Richardson, Jr. and Lewis W. Bender, in a classic ethnographic study of the academic cultures of two- and four-year institutions, concluded:

> [I]mproving opportunities for urban transfer students involves helping them adjust to two different kinds of institutions, each with its own set of values and basic assumptions. . . . The ways in which urban universities and community colleges view themselves and each other have significant implications for understanding the barriers that urban students must surmount in their pursuit of the baccalaureate degree.[6]

Richardson and Bender developed a taxonomy that identified seven areas where two- and four-year institutions differ in fundamental ways despite an overall focus on postsecondary education. The most important (for our purposes) include the following: "mission" (community colleges emphasize the specific needs of the surrounding community, while four-year institutions emphasize knowledge production); "functional priority" (community colleges privilege teaching while four-year institutions are more interested in faculty research); "student assumptions" (community colleges, lacking rigorous admissions requirements, are more likely to meet students "where they are" via remediation and other student academic support services, whereas four-year institutions more often see their students as independent learners); and "concept of quality" (community colleges advance egalitarianism and four-year institutions promote selectivity and elitism). These differences define each institution's core mission and, as a result, have an impact across a variety of academic and administrative policies and practices.

Analyzed in isolation, these differences are essential to each institution's definition of itself. For example, community college leaders pride themselves on the support systems they have developed to serve students. Faculty are evaluated primarily on their success as teachers (as opposed to researchers), and the curricula and pedagogy they create are directed toward student success and support, as evidenced, for instance, by a significant commitment to developmental education.

These characteristics are not unique to community colleges; they can be identified at other kinds of postsecondary institutions. Still, it is the community colleges' special charter to create an academic environment that welcomes all individuals regardless of their previous educational history and to focus on their educational success.

University leaders would be quick to respond that their institutions are also committed to effective instruction and student success, but they would, we think, acknowledge that faculty are more interested in conducting research or advancing scholarship generally than teaching. Faculty operate on an assumption, correctly or not, that most students who attend their institutions ought to be prepared largely to teach themselves.

At the very least, we can agree that students who are admitted to four-year institutions (research, liberal arts, and regional publics) are expected to be prepared for college-level work. As a result, teaching and pedagogy, though an important faculty function, are rated as less important compared to this function in community colleges and other open-access institutions.

Indeed, admissions requirements at four-year colleges and universities serve to raise the bar for those who wish to attend these institutions while reinforcing a system in which most student learning is highly individualistic. Moreover, the research enterprise at large public and private institutions often dictates large lower-division lecture courses, led by tenure-track, four-year institution faculty but staffed by graduate students who operate labs or discussion sections.

In this context, the most successful undergraduate students are those who employ strategies probably gained in highly resourced or competitive high schools, understanding that the key to success in a large research institution is to assert one's intellectual mettle rather early.

We agree that our description of faculty aims at two- and four-year institutions is broadly drawn to emphasize an important distinction between them. Given the diversity of US higher education institutions, we appreciate that readers are certain to identify examples of postsecondary institutions in which the overlap of faculty intentions and prerogatives is blurred.

A good many four-year institutions, for instance, admit all students who apply to their institutions, and, indeed, there are some community college programs in highly subscribed areas such as nursing where only the most academically prepared are admitted. Still, even if this was the case generally, we hold that the fundamental differences in faculty focus stem from the stated mission of these institutions and are, therefore, the *sine qua non* for the institution's existence.

That community college faculty are especially committed to teaching and pedagogy is mission-driven, because many of the students they serve are not well prepared for higher education. They are tasked with, in many cases, preparing students for college rather than advancing the academic success of students who already possess the foundational knowledge and skills to be successful in postsecondary education.

Such efforts are central to the community college, not as an afterthought or special case expressed as Herculean exceptionalism. Similarly, the focus of university faculty on knowledge generation has proven to be one of the greatest achievements of the American research university.[7] It is not, by definition, inherently less instructive or vital. It is different, however, from the mission of community colleges.

This gulf between two- and four-year institutions is rarely acknowledged, even if it is plainly evident. Indeed, the topic would not be especially interesting except when we consider the plight of a transfer student who must transcend both environments. Having been nurtured at the community college in small classes taught by instructors whose jobs depend on their teaching prowess, they move on to a new institution in which the focus is less on student success and more on the production of research.

Even the prosaic necessities of attending college present transfer students with some unique challenges. Transfer students will move from a relatively small institutional footprint to a four-year institution that is usually larger and more complex. They will discover transportation and housing to be a challenge, if only in comparison to the geographic convenience of the community college, which is almost always predicated on the assumption that students will live at home while attending college.

Transfer students will find that the favorable academic progress conditions they enjoyed at the two-year institution will be much different at the four-year university. For example, most community colleges do not generally monitor the academic progress of their students. Students can enroll and stop out at will, without any notification that they have failed to make necessary progress for an academic year.

Universities are far less forgiving, almost always mandating that students complete some number of credits annually. Although such a progress measure is unlikely to be strict, this will likely require the transfer student to attend continuously and full time, a state of commitment that is largely unrecognizable at community colleges, where 63 percent attend part time.[8]

Indeed, it is this commitment to full-time study that distinguishes the two institutions from one another in ways that may most profoundly affect the progress of transfer students. Yet they emanate from institutional missions, as Richardson and Bender highlight, that respond to historical priorities and aims.

MISSIONS AND MOTIVES

If the historical foundations of two- and four-institutions appear to have such an effect on transfer students today, it is important to articulate these long-held perspectives. As noted earlier, these institutions were conceived of in different centuries for different reasons. Are two- and four-year institutions focused on the same things? And if not, does the transfer pathway make sense academically?

Four-year colleges and universities have followed what has come to be known at the German system.[9] Under this model, the professor and her research are the center of this intellectual universe. While serving the needs of undergraduates, the hierarchy of these institutions values research above all else, and it looks to engage only the best and the brightest students to be a part of this work.

Many of the colleges and research universities in the United States sought this elite moniker, advancing institutional prestige, research prowess, and faculty distinction as the cornerstones of their institutional worldview. To be sure, there are many four-year institutions whose allegiance to this kind of elite, historical traditional is tenuous at best. But the traditions remain.

Core elements of almost every four-year institution in the United States incorporate such long-standing characteristics as tenure, shared governance, knowledge generation, and selective admission requirements, all of which place the faculty at the center of the institution's mission and decision-making. The four-year institutional mission is driven primarily by the collective work of the individuals who are at the center of this universe: the faculty member and her classroom.

As noted earlier, the earliest history of community colleges was guided, among others, by elite institutional leaders who were interested in expanding postsecondary-education access generally while making their own institutions more selective. The professed desire was to accommodate a growing number of students seeking credentials beyond high school as the Industrial Revolution and political populism took full flower in the early nineteenth century.

University leaders did not start the community college movement alone, however. They were aided significantly by local K–12 school leaders, who saw an opportunity to extend the high school curriculum by two years; by community boosters who appreciated the economic and cultural benefits that a college, even a small one, could offer; and by state politicians guided even then by a desire to provide educational opportunity to his or her constituents at a reasonable cost.[10]

At the start, the mission of the community college was transfer. This predominance is sometimes lost in contemporary treatments of community college "origins," but the historical record could not be clearer.[11] Although vocational programs played a role in the early community college curriculum, their influence was modest compared to the offerings in the liberal arts. However, the historical record also reveals a significant shift in emphasis from transfer to vocational and workforce training, beginning in the early 1930s.

The Great Depression was a motivating factor; training individuals for immediate employment did not need to be rationalized. Nevertheless, the seeds of departure from traditional higher education had been planted by national community college leaders.

William Eells, one of the first presidents of the American Association of Junior Colleges, highlighted the voice of advocates who believed that the future of community colleges could be most profitably ensured through the development of terminal degrees and vocational education, rather than dependence on four-year institutions via the transfer pathway. In his book, *Present Status of Junior College Terminal Education*, he quotes several junior college presidents—the example below being most representative:

> I wonder if the junior colleges are going to take over this program of fitting people to live, or are just preparatory institutions to the four-year colleges and universities; whether we are going to assert our right to a "place in the sun" to serve men and women, fitting them for life at that level, or whether we are just going to be a tail for the universities to wag.[12]

Although some students would be qualified to move on, most would be interested in the kinds of workforce training that would lead to immediate employment after college. Indeed, entire community college systems were developed as experiments in vocational training, often referred to as technical colleges. These colleges and systems often offered the kinds of liberal arts courses one might find at a traditional four-year institution, but the focus—in curricula, facilities, and outlook—was clearly devoted to workforce preparation.

This focus has remained steady throughout the history of community colleges, creating a tension between the goals of the liberal arts, as reflected in the baccalaureate degree, and those of the marketplace, as reflected in vocational education.

Even if "transfer" is included in the mission of a two-year college, the commitment to that process is sometimes tentative. For their part, four-year colleges and universities often use this as a reason to refrain from articulating courses with local community colleges, offering the rationale that the mission of their institution is simply too distinct (or discrepant) from the community college. We will have more to say about this in the "Credit and Credibility" section below.

POPULISM AND ELITISM

The different historical trajectories and divergent missions of two- and four-year institutions play out most obviously in the conditions of admission for both institutions. Community colleges are open-access institutions; for all intents and purposes, everyone who applies to these institutions is admitted. In the absence of admissions requirements, even basic college-readiness is a phrase that might mean nothing more than the ability to pass a placement test in arithmetic or English grammar.

This degree of access, however, is the community colleges' reason for existence, the most majestic representation of its democratic and populist roots. It is an extraordinary vision of higher education as a place that supports educational advancement for all who have the willingness to apply themselves in the work of earning a postsecondary credential.

Contrast this egalitarianism with that of four-year colleges and universities in the United States. Although many of these institutions have only the most minimal of admissions requirements, there is at least a common notion that students who wish to attend these institutions must be "college-ready."

Inherent in this perspective is the idea that college represents not simply a graded, stepped relationship from high school but a leap in educational commitment and academic rigor. As a result, applicants to these institutions are required to complete a series of college-preparatory courses in high school in such traditional disciplines as English, mathematics, arts and humanities, and the physical, life, and social sciences.

Community college advocates will argue that differences in entrance requirements between their institutions and four-year colleges and universities is a matter of degree, not substance; they will say that open-access admissions policies and admissions selectivity are not discrete academic universes but represent part of the same intellectual continuum. In the abstract, this contention sounds convincing, but as a practical matter, it misses the competitive challenge that transfer students face when they step onto a four-year campus.

In 2018, Harvard and Princeton universities admitted less than 10 percent of all their applicants. Even a public flagship like the University of California, Los Angeles reported an admit rate well under 20 percent. As college has increased in popularity, more and more institutions are selecting students among large and increasingly competitive first-year student applicant pools. The result, especially for the most popular institutions, is the need to raise standards of admission for transfer students as the university selects entrants among a pool of at least minimally qualified applicants.

In terms of academic competition, it becomes increasingly difficult to make a persuasive argument that community college students in, say, an introductory biology class will be pushed as hard intellectually as students in the same class at a four-year college and university.

We know that student engagement is one of the most critical elements of effective learning. If one's peers are pivotal in advancing individual learning, should we be surprised that the community college classroom—despite the often-heralded commitment of that segment to teaching and pedagogy—should be considered fundamentally different than that of the four-year university classroom?

This is not to deride the potential and work ethic of community college students (nor to overstate the motivation of students attending four-year universities). Still, a classroom full of students who have attended well-resourced high schools, participated in one or more standardized test-prep courses, and completed a battery of AP courses must be a higher base from which to learn than a classroom whose participants needed nothing other to enter the class than bus fare.[13]

Whereas community colleges, in the most democratic manifestation of their mission, continue to admit students with the widest variation in academic abilities, four-year institutions are increasingly put-upon to admit students with higher and higher levels of academic achievement. Were two- and four-year institutions never to interact administratively, differences in selectivity and student preparation would not matter.

But when the focus is turned to transfer, how do we square the desire of community college students who attend an open-access institution with the intention to transfer with the fact that the very institutions to which they wish to enroll regularly turn away thousands of students with stronger academic credentials?

It does not matter materially that most community college students never get admitted to Harvard—most first-year students don't either. The initial equation is problematic. How do we create pathways among two fundamentally different institutions, pathways that make sense academically and can fairly accommodate students who wish to traverse the two- and four-year academic environments?

If you believe that this discussion about differences in admission requirements is overstated, we need look no further than the example of four-year institutions with more stringent requirements for applicants from two-year institutions. Some four-year institutions require that community college transfer applicants present higher GPAs than their four-year counterparts. The University of California, for example, requires transfer students from California community colleges to earn at least a 2.40 GPA for admission to any of its campuses, implying that a "C" average (2.00) is insufficient preparation for a student to come from one postsecondary-education institution to another.

A four-year institution's rationale for these different academic thresholds is generally linked to concerns about ensuring that two-year students are well-prepared for the rigors of the upper-division after transfer. Community college advocates argue that disparate treatment signals a sentimental and somewhat paternalist view of community colleges and the students that attend these institutions.

They go on to note that a considerable body of research reveals few differences between the eventual success of transfer students following their move to a four-year institution regardless of their collegiate origins. Yet can we blame four-year institutional leaders who are suspicious of the academic rigor of community colleges, given the range of ability among the students that community colleges admit?

So long as an institutional higher education hierarchy persists in which one type of institution is viewed as superior to another, there can be no true accord between two- and four-year institutions, only suspicion that the intellect and even the fortitude of community college students cannot measure up to the world of students who attend four-year institutions. For students with baccalaureate aspirations, this is lethal.

CREDIT AND CREDIBILITY

The issue that bedevils transfer students most directly is the extent to which they may transfer course credit from one institution to another. In higher education, there are few issues that anger the public and its elected representatives more significantly than the failure of two- and four-year institutions to accept one another's courses for credit.

It is especially galling to legislators when this occurs among public postsecondary-education institutions, where there is a reasonable expectation that tax dollars supporting the curriculum of public postsecondary institutions ought to be fully portable. If all money is green, shouldn't all college courses be equal?

More distressing, however, is the idea that higher education institutions do not, simply on their face, accept one another's curricula without question. Would it not be appropriate to expect a kind of professional courtesy that includes a respect for the quality of courses offered, the pedagogy associated with the delivery of those courses, and the faculty who designed them? Yet transfer students are often surprised to learn when they matriculate at the four-year institution that they must take additional courses or repeat courses they completed at a community college.

In a comprehensive review of credit transfer, the first large-scale study of its kind, the US Government Accountability Office (GAO) issued a set of findings in 2017 that revealed what many transfer students already knew: the portability of course credit from one institution to another is neither certain nor smooth.[14]

The GAO's longitudinal study of student course-taking over six years revealed not only that colleges and universities place barriers on the number and kind of courses they will accept for degree credit but also that transfer students have a difficult time finding this out prior to transfer so that they can prepare themselves effectively.

Overall, the GAO reported that up to 30 percent of all transferred courses needed to be retaken by students who had transferred from one institution to another and that "Students lost an estimated 43 percent of college credit when they transferred, or an estimated 13 credits, on average." Credit loss by institution varied. Students who transferred between public institutions lost about lost 37 percent of their credit. And students who transferred vertically—that is, transferred from a two-year institution to a four-year institution—lost about 22 percent of their credit.

Of course, there are justifiable reasons why certain courses would not be applied to a student's major. A student's completion of courses in the welding arts is unlikely to be looked upon favorably by a nursing school. It makes perfect sense for the nursing school to reject an applicant who is unprepared for its course of study.

Still, the larger question is why two- and four-year institutions fail to address this concern in any systematic way, often encouraging politicians and policymakers to implement their own meat-cleaver approaches, such as common course numbering, which labels courses but offers nothing in the way of quality control.

RESOURCES AND REVENUES

The final contradiction relates to the ways in which two- and four-year institutions are supported. The gap between what community colleges receive from state governments compared to what four-year institutions receive is significant. Community colleges, though enrolling 43 percent of the undergraduates in America, receive only about one-third of the support as compared to public four-year colleges and universities.[15] Moreover, according to the College Board, community colleges charge on average, only one-third of the tuition and fees as compared to four-year colleges and universities.[16]

Both types of institutions often make convincing cases for the expense of their operations, the appropriations they solicit from state and local coffers, the fees they charge to students, and, in the case of most four-year institutions, the overhead they demand to conduct research on their campuses. For example, the overhead associated with sustaining the research enterprise at four-year colleges and universities is significant, but it is rationalized as an investment that repays itself multiple times over in the currency of knowledge discovery. This output is not insubstantial.

Four-year institutions often—and rightly—tout the accomplishments of their faculty in all disciplines. Careful commenters on the productivity of research universities have documented the economic impact of these accomplishments in the regional and national economy, highlighted advances in the arts and sciences that generate new cultural wealth in communities, and linked research directly to boosts in the well-being of the nation's citizenry.[17]

These advances require significant and sustained investment, and it would be hard to make a claim that such research and development be undermined especially when the benefits are so clearly manifest in the life and culture of the United States.

For their part, community college advocates argue that their institutions represent an investment in human capital formation of the most critical kind: the training of individuals who might not otherwise be prepared for the workplace, and the opportunity for them to have jobs that provide family-sustaining wages.

Both regional and national economies benefit from an educated workforce. Community college leaders understand that, though the research conducted at universities is a pivotal part of a healthy economy, creating a workforce that translates this knowledge generation into productive outputs is also key.

Postsecondary education at all levels is, clearly, a productive and cost-effective societal investment. The contradiction for our purposes, however, is how much less community colleges receive as compared to baccalaureate-granting institutions.

Support-level variation between two- and four-year institutions can be traced to long-standing differences in the types of funding streams used to pay for their operations. In the public sector, community colleges and four-year institutions receive substantial parts of their revenue from state appropriations. But four-year institutions also receive a significant portion of their revenue from other, more diverse sources.

Research institutions often bring in substantial federal grants and contracts, and others generate revenue through medical or other health-care related services. Public and private colleges and universities also rely substantially on tuition. Since the Great Recession in 2008–09, tuition at public four-year colleges and universities now accounts for more than 50 percent of their revenue, an outcome that has led many public-institution leaders to quip that their schools are "state-located," not "state-supported."

These differences in revenue streams can be easily seen on any budget analyst's spreadsheet, but it is the relatively recent reliance on tuition that has exacerbated the divide in support between two- and four-year institutions. Given the focus on open admission, community colleges are reluctant to increase tuition levels, believing that such a move will reduce access to their programs and services by low-income students. This reluctance, however, has other costs:

> The educational philosophy that guides community colleges requires them to strive to enroll all who seek admission, but many community college leaders and other observers worry that resources are being stretched beyond the point where quality and opportunity begin to suffer.[18]

Other observers make the case that the strain on community colleges to serve the most challenged students with the fewest resources is well past the breaking point and is costing the nation dearly. As Andrew S. Rosen concludes in his book *Change.edu: Rebooting for the New Talent Economy*:

> [Community colleges] are operating with a financial model that's fundamentally broken. They are highly-dependent on (widely variable) state budgets for most of their funding, and are often deeply reluctant to ask students to contribute much money to their own education. Very low price, however, does not mean very low cost. . . . As state legislators became painfully aware during the Great Recession, taxpayer resources aren't unlimited.[19]

Maintaining an open-enrollment policy in the face of reduced or inadequate resources ensures access, but not authentic opportunity. Without needed class sections, faculty labor, counseling, and academic support services, the open door of the community college may lead nowhere for many students.

As noted earlier, four-year college advocates—especially those associated with research-intensive institutions—will advance the argument that meeting their mission requires greater investments, but the benefits that accrue from those investments pay long-term dividends. They might also suggest that community college leaders tear a page from the four-year institution playbook by committing themselves to a high-tuition/high-aid model. More tuition revenue will provide the resources to supply academic support for students.

Indeed, one could argue that the resources are already available to make this happen in the form of Pell Grants. California, for example, which charges community college students the lowest tuition prices in the nation, rarely collects the Pell Grant fee dollars that it could legitimately if a high-tuition/high-aid model was adopted.

Community college advocates are rightfully suspicious, however, of raising rates on students whose annual incomes might make it impossible for them to access higher education, even though its poorest students would be able to attend college full-time. Yet access to community colleges absent the resources necessary for them to help students achieve their educational goals would seem a cruel kind of bait and switch.

It is ironic—or simply a cynical ploy—that the politicians most enamored of community colleges are those that see them simply as inexpensive ways of housing students who might be otherwise unskilled. That is a harsh assessment, but there is a difference between the appeal of open access and the challenge of making such an enterprise work:

> Politicians like to give speeches and voice support for community colleges because they like the spirit of the All-Access Playbook under which such schools operate. At the same time, the legislators who write the checks are aware of the struggles students have at these schools to reach graduation, and even today some wonder if the ideal of universal postsecondary education is realistic—whether all students should be considered "college material." They'll fund community colleges to the extent that it's politically necessary, but no further.[20]

Community colleges are almost always asked to pick up the slack of the K–12 systems graduates who are not ready for college or work. The growing problem of remedial education in higher education is at least an outgrowth of failures in secondary education.

Community colleges' open-access policy provides the entrée for students who in any other country might well never make it to higher education. They have authentic needs, but community colleges—the lowest rung on the higher educational hierarchy—almost always lack sufficient funding to serve these most challenged students.

SUMMARY

The differences we have described in this chapter between two- and four-year institutions, whatever their historical origins and present-day proclivities, prove problematic only when students attempt to cross these institutional boundaries, and they appear to be no less problematic even when such crossings, in the form of transfer, have been publicly sanctioned by state and federal laws and guidelines and been publicly agreed to by participating institutions.

From a student-service perspective, institutional differences matter in fundamental ways. Institutional worldviews are translated by administrators and faculty into practices that shape student attitudes toward college and their ability to complete a postsecondary credential.

That there are differences—significant ones—between community colleges and four-year colleges and universities is not at issue in this chapter. That these differences drive institutional culture, administrative policy, and professional practice is also self-evident to any observer of the US higher education landscape. Even the idea that such differences signal value-laden expectations for students, their families, faculty, administrators, and policymakers is also to miss the disjuncture at the center of the transfer pathway.

The heart of the matter is not simply to recite these differences, but to understand the corrosive aspect of their oppositional impact on students who begin at community colleges with a desire to earn a baccalaureate degree, and who are stymied by contradictions that appear, like the monolith in *2001: A Space Odyssey*, as faceless, nameless, unknowable, and abstract.

These contradictions are not abstract; they could not be more concrete, possessing measurable effects on a pathway that was designed with the intention of expanding higher education access. Recognizing and then addressing them, with the full appreciation of the diversity and history of two- and four-year institutions, is a reasonable first step in strengthening transfer and propelling the students whose earnest desire is to travel a pathway that leads to educational success.

Chapter 2

The Flickering and Largely Untold History of Transfer

"The habit of moving from one institution to another is beginning to gain ground . . . and when thoroughly considered it is a custom the advantages of which cannot be denied. Hundreds and hundreds of students, I might perhaps say thousands, find it to their advantage, for one reason or another, to spend a portion of their college life in one institution and another portion in another."

—William Rainey Harper, *The Prospects of the Small College*[1]

The transfer pathway is not ahistorical, but it is often treated that way. In histories of higher education in the United States, the transfer function is dealt with in fits and starts, and mostly as part of a broader description of community colleges. This is not unfair, but it is inadequate. And even when scholars attempt to describe this pathway, the process is usually portrayed as merely a singular transactional act, something that students *do* rather than something they *are*.

This characterization hardly resembles the behavior of many students in US higher education today. More than ever, "student swirl"—the irregular and almost random ways in which students cobble together degrees by attending multiple institutions—is becoming the accepted standard practice of college-going in America.

But transfer represents something special about access to higher education in the United States. For many students, it is a transformative higher education pivot point. It often elevates students who never dreamed of earning a four-year degree, equipping them with a credential that is a ticket to broader economic and cultural opportunities. Today's discussion of swirling students is a hollow echo of what transfer was supposed to represent and what it was designed to offer any student from modest means with the grit and guts to go to college.

When we forget or do not acknowledge the historical levers that created the transfer pathway, we are potentially unfaithful to higher education's commitment to access and equity. We also threaten our contemporary understanding of transfer, including its contradictions and failures, as we described in chapter 1.

If we believe that transfer is, or should be, a higher education access point for many students, it can only be authentically evaluated when we understand the motivations and aspirations of the early founders who developed the transfer pathway. In sowing the seeds of transfer over a century ago, those founders set the stage for the triumph and failures we observe in various forms of transfer today.

Of course, a single chapter cannot do justice to the history that is transfer. Other scholars have tackled this topic and filled gaps we will not address here. There are at least two seminal books that treat the traditional transfer process with the dignity and scholarship it deserves: *The Diverted Dream: Community Colleges and the Promise of Educational Opportunity in America, 1900–1985,* by Steven Brint and Jerome Karabel;[2] and *The Contradictory College: The Conflicting Origins, Impacts, and Futures of the Community College,* by Kevin J. Dougherty.[3]

Both books, now several decades old, are sometimes criticized by community college advocates because they paint an occasionally negative portrait of that segment's commitment to transfer students. Despite this, we recommend that you find copies and read them both.

Even if you disagree with the authors' conclusions, their scholarship is airtight. Both books are a goldmine of rich and detailed research that illuminates a largely unstudied history of American higher education. More recently, additional writers and scholars have brought perspective to this important topic, such as J. M. Beach's *Gateway to Opportunity? A History of the Community College in the United States*[4] and Arthur M. Cohen and Florence B. Brawer's *The American Community College.*[5]

In this chapter, our purpose is to build on the work of these scholars. Despite our narrowed focus, we strive to locate the transfer horizon line by describing its origin story for clues to help us forecast its future. In this way, too, we wish to illustrate transfer as a topic worthy unto itself: a pivotal marker of students' transformation educationally, and a pathway that will increasingly characterize the experience of students in the twenty-first century.

WHO "INVENTED" TRANSFER?

It would be foolish to name a single individual as the catalyst for the creation of the traditional transfer pathway. The idea of a "junior" college is often credited to Henry P. Tappan, president of the University of Michigan in the 1850s.[6] There is also general agreement that Joliet Junior College in Illinois, established in 1901, is the first public institution of this type, an innovation championed by William Rainey Harper, president of the University of Chicago, and J. Stanley Brown, principle of Joliet High School in Illinois.[7]

In the treatment to follow, we privilege Harper's contributions to the transfer pathway, albeit understanding that other educational leaders did play a role then and subsequently in what we now call the transfer pathway. Our rationale is Harper's visionary language, which startles and amazes us for its contemporary relevance about the need for a new higher education hierarchy in the United States.

At the time of his untimely death at age 50 in 1906, Harper was remarkably prescient about the needs of a modern America that was only beginning to benefit economically from the Industrial Revolution. Beyond his administration of one of America's most elite private institutions and his own scholarly efforts in the history of religion, Harper's view of US higher education is surely the most stirring and coherent testament of higher education's value in addressing the needs of America's democracy:

> Education, indeed, must be the first and foremost policy of democracy. It is the foundation which underlies all else. . . . It is the university that, as the center of thought, is to maintain for democracy the unity so essential for its success.[8]

For Harper, American postsecondary education should consist of at least two main elements. Large, well-financed research universities would instruct only the best students in the final two years of what he called the "upper-division," reflecting the junior and senior classes of today. Junior colleges would offer instruction in the "lower-division," or the first two years of college.[9] Harper indicates that some (but not all) students would move from the lower-division to the upper-division, today's modern equivalent of what we call lateral transfer.

Harper does not dwell on how students would be selected for transfer, but a fair reading of his work indicates that only students who excelled at the junior college would be invited to the four-year institution. Students so qualified to transfer to a four-year institution would reap the benefits, in Harper's view, of a well-supported research institution that would not only confer the baccalaureate degree but also open the possibility of additional advancement in graduate or professional school.

But what of students who did not qualify or who were not invited to transfer to these senior institutions? Harper believed that these students would benefit from the additional years of schooling they received in the junior college. For those students, the completion of two additional years would earn them what Harper called an "associate's certificate," the forerunner of today's associate's degree:

> With the completion of the two-year course a certificate is given, granting the title of "associate" in the university. . . . The provision of a two-year course meets the needs of many who cannot take a longer term of residence, and likewise of many who ought not to take a longer course.[10]

Although Harper is credited as one of the founders of the junior college and as identifying a pathway for transfer between two- and four-year institutions, his primary motivation for doing so may have been located elsewhere. Harper was focused on making elite universities more elite, even as he worked to develop a system that would provide a steady stream of talent preparing for these special, but exclusive, places.

Seemingly a progressive politically, Harper was also a product of his time, a public intellectual who was deeply committed to the value of scholarly and scientific research. Yet his worldview could only be accomplished through the development of a limited number of large, well-financed universities whose students would represent the very best of the nation's intellectual capital.

Harper's celebration of research universities and his engineering of a transfer function as a kind of peripheral use in support of these universities is not to imply that his vision for postsecondary education was narrow. He seems to embrace the gospel of higher education for all who might benefit from its opportunities. His vision is consistent with the progressives of his time, promoting the potential and success of all individuals who could prove their mettle intellectually:

> The university is an institution of the people. It must, therefore, be "privileged" and in many instances supported by the people. . . . The university touches life, every phase of life, at every point. . . . The university is of the people, and for the people, whether considered individually or collectively.[11]

However problematic Harper's position might have been in 1905 (women did not have the right to vote, the nation was only four decades removed from the Civil War, and the challenges of DACA students were not yet in the news), Harper's professed intention was—authentically—to increase opportunity to higher education rather than to restrict it.

Harper's Rationale

To understand better how the transfer process came to be in America and to appreciate its advantages and disadvantages today, we need to understand Harper's rationale for the creation of junior colleges and transfer. There is similarity between Harper's time and our own regarding the ways in which higher education was applied as a "means of ascent" for individuals from all socioeconomic backgrounds.[12]

Like many other progressives of this period, Harper understood that expanding education was key to the success of democracy and its economic well-being. Although the compulsory high school was not yet three decades old in Harper's day, it demonstrated that additional education was desired by a great many Americans and that the economic and cultural life of the nation would be improved.

In Harper's America, large, elite research institutions—financially well-endowed and the center of America's scholarly and scientific prowess—were relatively rare. Although President Abraham Lincoln's Morrill Act helped establish some of the great public universities of today, the result of the Land Grant movement, such as California, Michigan, and Wisconsin, were only beginning to be felt.

Even though renowned private institutions such as Harvard, Princeton, and Stanford had by Harper's time emerged as the guardians of a uniquely American educational elitism, higher education in the United States was dominated at the turn of the twentieth century by small colleges. These institutions were a patchwork of insufficiently funded institutions, as described by Harper, each enrolling a few hundred students and usually linked to a religious order or denomination. Although Harper was sympathetic to the original founding of these small colleges, he believed they had outlived their usefulness:

> Much of the work formerly done by the colleges is now being done by the high schools. The course of study in many high schools is more extensive and more thorough than was the course of study in many of the better colleges thirty or forty years ago.[13]

But what kind of higher education structure should replace these small colleges? Harper was clear on this point. He believed that the great scholarly and scientific questions of the new century could only be addressed by a limited number of well-supported research institutions.

Smaller four-year colleges and universities simply did not have the resources—the faculty, the libraries, and the laboratories—to engage in the kind of full-scale research enterprise that was required.[14] Better, he argued, to close many of these colleges or reorient their focus in ways that would provide additional education to those individuals who wished to move beyond high school but not earn a four-year degree.

That degree, the baccalaureate, in his view, should be the rightful province of larger, well-resourced research institutions. Moreover, Harper was agnostic about whether additional education for the US student population should be two years added to the high school curriculum or offered separately at a junior college. Harper saw little academic distinction between the end of high school and the start of college, arguing that the most important intellectual divide came between the sophomore and junior years:

> The higher work of the university will be separated more clearly from the lower work of the college; many colleges will undertake to do work of a more distinctively college character than that which they are now doing; and many high schools will rise to the grade and dignity of colleges. . . . Only a few institutions will endeavor to cover the entire ground.[15]

Harper's academic demarcation between the sophomore and junior years offered a new kind of higher education hierarchy in the United States. This hierarchy would consist of junior colleges—as extensions of comprehensive high schools or separate entities unto themselves—along with research-intensive institutions that would offer instruction in the junior and senior years, providing a launching point for students wishing to go on to graduate or professional school.[16]

As noted earlier, Harper's enthusiasm for this new hierarchy was probably designed to highlight and advance the aims of his University of Chicago and similarly endowed institutions rather than to promote junior colleges. His reasoning, however, was sound. Anticipating—correctly—that the explosion of scientific knowledge would be an expensive one to support, Harper believed that the establishment of large institutions would be a better model to advance this work.

Borrowing this approach from successful European university models, Harper sought to drain resources away from the patchwork of small, independent, and insufficiently funded small colleges in support of relatively few four-year research institutions and junior colleges. Only then, Harper argued, would the United States be able to compete with the likes of foreign powers in Great Britain, France, and Germany, which boasted world-famous and elite centers of learning and scholarship.

But Harper appears to be as pragmatic as he was progressive. He knew that to garner the support for his position, he would need to advocate for greater access to postsecondary education for Americans, citing the popularity of compulsory high school in the United States as evidence.[17] He went on to note that academies and other kinds of college-preparatory schools had begun to lose students to the high schools, asserting that high school curricula would begin to tackle subjects normally found in the first year of college.

Harper's answer was not to abandon small colleges but to reorder their priorities to the first two years of college rather than a program of four years. Cleverly, his rationale did not rely solely on the argument that these small colleges lacked the resources to adequately train students for the four-year degree; rather, he believed that the obvious advantages of small colleges—lower overhead, smaller classes, and locally available—were key to an America whose citizens hungered for more education:

> As long as there are families with small incomes, and as long as in these families there are sons and daughters who desire a higher education, there must be colleges in which this education may be obtained at a minimum of expense. The future of the small college is, therefore, absolutely assured.[18]

What he did not say directly, but which is an essential link in his argument, was that the research institutions he envisioned would need a steady supply of talented and hard-working students to fill the libraries and laboratories and to become the future members of the faculty. Junior colleges could serve that function by preparing students in the lower-division for the important work they might undertake in the upper-division. By eliminating competition from small colleges that offered four-year degrees, research institutions would be free to flourish unfettered.

The Outcomes of Harper's Grand Hierarchy

This short description of the transfer origin story provides the framework we seek in discussing contemporary transfer issues. We have touched only briefly on the roots of transfer; arguably, other policymakers, visionaries, and critics had a greater influence than Harper on the trajectory of this educational pathway. But our conceit in focusing on Harper's perspective is that his grand design aids us in grappling with transfer's next era, forcing us to consider questions that his vision raised but never answered—or simply deferred altogether.

What Did Harper Get Right?

The historical legitimacy of any prominent figure is rarely the result of that individual's prescience in predicting the future correctly in every detail; nor does historical longevity require that his or her vision be verified as the cause of some future outcome. It need only come to pass when the individual's vision aligns with that future in the most general of ways.

Although Harper's vision is not identical to current US educational structure, his prognostications about a growing thirst for education by regular

Americans, the need in the form of additional years of instruction after high school, and US dominance in the production of research and of research institutions were remarkably accurate.

It is unlikely that even Harper could have predicted that his proposal for the creation of junior colleges would have resulted in an astonishing proliferation of two-year community colleges. Today, 1,200 community colleges enroll 43 percent of all undergraduates in the United States, one of the largest higher education segments in the country.[19] Geographically convenient, relatively low-cost, and open to anyone who might benefit, these institutions could not be more in tune with the egalitarian spirit of democratic America.

Although elite research institutions still garner a disproportionate share of federal and state funding, community colleges educate far more students, especially those who might not otherwise have access to higher education. This component remains essential to all of the various forms of transfer found today.

Harper's second bullseye was his advocacy of the need for American research universities—well-funded, focused on the big issues of science mostly but scholarship generally, and interested in admitting only the very best students. These public and private institutions are still a blueprint being copied by other countries that wish to compete globally in an increasingly competitive international search for a talented workforce.

Of course, Harper did not invent or influence the transformative growth and success of Land Grant institutions, the Ivy League schools, or any other four-year university system. But his singular devotion to the idea of these institutions provided a broad framework for others to implement.

Finally, and most centrally for our discussion here, Harper anticipated the need for an academic pathway that would allow students to continue their educational journey after high school. Despite the fact that Harper did not dwell on the transfer pathway extensively, he understood early that a yearning for postsecondary instruction was brewing among many Americans and that new structures and institutions would need to be developed to accommodate them.

It is possible that Harper only intended to build a pipeline of well-prepared students to fill his research institutions. Implicit in Harper's writings is the idea that transfer would be a special case involving, probably, relatively few students: the best of the best.

Even if this position represents an inchoate elitism on his part, Harper also stressed a populist notion that any student could earn his way to the senior institution. Then, as today, Harper's suggestion that only some students would transfer was based on the practical notion that there would not be space among a relatively few research institutions to accommodate every junior college student, and, as a result, some limiting mechanism would need to be employed.

Although it would be inappropriate to grant Harper too much credit in how the transfer pathway ultimately evolved, he nevertheless coined an innovation that even today remains exceptional for those students who successfully travel this road. Transfer has no analog internationally; the prevailing European model, for example, is to track students from an early age into pre-set academic pathways.

From the beginning, the American ideal has been to advance the idea that individuals may continue their postsecondary schooling wherever their ambitions and hard work might lead them.

What Did Harper Miss?

He missed quite a lot, as it turns out. But those misperceptions illuminate— almost as effectively as his good guesses—aspects of transfer that we have yet to fully reckon with, and, as a result, they provide guideposts for improving the process for all students.

First on the docket of mislaid ideas is Harper's quaint notion that the network of US elite research institutions would offer only upper-division courses and graduate programs. A century ago—like today—university leaders could ill afford to forgo student fees at the first-year and sophomore levels. Those incoming students were needed to sustain expensive upper-division classes and seminars and to pay for graduate education.

Supporting graduate students by having them help teach lower-division courses has been an important leverage point for four-year institutions to support the research activities they so covet. Despite Harper's belief that the lower-division was probably better thought of as an extension of high school, both public and private four-year universities developed four-year baccalaureate degrees that have become the most popular model of postsecondary education in the United States.

Without a clear and unique set of responsibilities for two- and four-year institutions, competition for students was the inevitable result, with transfer students the inadvertent cast-offs. Although some have argued that research universities and community colleges do not compete for the same type of students, largely because they differ significantly in terms of admissions requirements, transfer suffers nonetheless.[20]

Research universities do not need transfer students to sustain their graduate programs. Even if they wished to admit transfer students—and many do— their ability to use these students to leverage and promote graduate education never rises to the level of importance of first-year students. And even if they do admit them, perhaps due to an insufficiently robust first-year enrolled class, it is largely for tactical rather than strategic reasons.

Transfer students are unattractive at other kinds of four-year institutions as well. Liberal arts colleges find that the allure of the four-year degree is precious enough to refuse to admit transfer students in any significant numbers. Curricula coherence is the often-used mantra to refrain from enrolling students midstream.

If Harper was right that there is a substantive difference in the intellectual approach and rigor of the lower- and upper-divisions, then the appearance of the transfer students as juniors should pose no special encumbrance for admission in the middle of the four-year degree. Nevertheless, the four-year baccalaureate model has provided senior institutions with a ready-made excuse not to admit transfer students, an attitude that dampens the legitimacy of the transfer pathway for students.[21]

A serious outgrowth of this attitude is a second trend Harper missed, or hoped would improve, which was the degree to which colleges and universities would cooperate with one another in ways that would advance American democracy and the educational aims of students:

> Yet a further change will be the development [in his system of organization] of a spirit of cooperation. It is only within a few years that there has been any cooperation worth mentioning among colleges and universities and the cooperation which has so far been inaugurated is of an exceedingly superficial character.[22]

For over a hundred years, the transfer process has offered two- and four-year institutions a singular opportunity to test this important goal. For the transfer process to work well, both educational segments must be full partners in the process. Community colleges must prepare students well for the demands of the upper-division. In turn, four-year institutions must admit community college students with a commitment that is something more than an afterthought spurred by an unsuccessful first-year recruitment cycle.

The degree to which this partnership has foundered, however, is apparent to transfer advocates at two- and four-year institutions. Four-year institutions hinder the transfer process by not accepting coursework from community colleges, often applying reasoning that is unassailable intellectually: open-access institutions are, by design, insufficiently rigorous to prepare students for success in the upper-division. And perhaps that is so, though the research evidence indicates that transfer students do as well as first-year students after transfer.

Even if this were universally true, however, the obligation of the four-year institution to transfer students cannot be so easily dismissed. If community college students do struggle academically after transfer, the four-year institution ought to identify those areas where student weaknesses exist and work with community colleges to close those gaps.

Course alignment and assessment of rigor are difficult challenges but are essential for a transfer partnership to flourish. To do anything less is to acknowledge that a kind of transfer glass ceiling exists for students who harbor transfer intentions to elite institutions.

Community colleges are not blameless, either. Data reveal that two-year institutions, very much like four-year institutions, construct significant barriers when it comes to students who wish to apply credit toward certificates and degrees from other institutions.[23] Students applying to four-year institutions from community colleges were denied credit for 22 percent of their credits. This jumps to 69 percent, however, when students attempt to transfer credit between two-year institutions. The incentive of institutions to privilege their own curriculum over the academic enterprise conducted elsewhere is not unique to four-year institutions.[24]

We cannot be too critical that Harper missed the complexity of the credit transfer process in contemporary American higher education, especially since so few students were mobile in America at that time. He did, however, anticipate that transfer would become increasingly important to more students, and that such transfer was likely to involve students moving from smaller institutions to universities:

> Impelled by a desire to go out into the larger world, led by the reputation of some great teacher or investigator, driven perhaps by the necessity of earning his livelihood, or forced by reason of the removal of the family home, the student finds his way to the university and finishes the work begun in the small college.[25]

That we today have still not found a good solution to the problem of credit transfer continues to hinder a full realization of the transfer pathway. That this issue is complex, involving a variety of self-interested constituencies, is to labor what was obvious to Harper: education should serve democracy and students.

The final trend that Harper missed—reflecting the fact that even his astonishing vision was limited—was the extraordinary popularity of the transfer process itself for first-time community college students. Most first-time students who begin their college careers at two-year institutions dream of earning a baccalaureate degree.[26]

Seeing that access promoted by the local college, and hearing the lofty pronouncements of four-year leaders about transfer students, they pursue their aim with a reasonable expectation that the pathway between two- and four-year institutions is at least a highway paved with something more than good intentions.

Despite their enthusiasm, however, the desires of most students are not fulfilled. We write elsewhere in this book about why this may be so, but the essential fact is that, though most new college students who enter a community college wish to transfer, the vast majority do not. Dougherty's harsh evaluation almost three decades ago rings true today:

> [I]t is important to underscore the finding that community college students— even if we restrict our focus to baccalaureate aspirants—secure significantly fewer baccalaureate degrees than four-year entrants.[27]

The question for us is whether students' transfer expectations constitute failure or are the logical outcome of an open-access system that receives the most challenged students with the fewest resources to support them. In Harper's day, the fact that *any* college student could, with the requisite amount of determination and persistence, transfer to the senior institution was the celebratory moment, not that *all* students who desire that outcome would achieve it.

In fact, we have an entire dominion of research focused on the extent to which two-year institutions serve as "democracy's college"—in other words, they are meant to structure failure by "cooling out" students' expectations and directing them to vocational options that are better aligned with their skills and the aims of local businesses.[28]

The reality seems to be that we lack a definition of failure for students who begin college at a two-year institution. In Harper's conception, he was clear that only a minority of students would ever transfer to the upper-division. In Harper's day, compulsory high school was in its infancy. In 1899–1900, only 3.3 percent of all students enrolled in primary or secondary education attended a high school.[29]

That a majority of students never transferred cannot be seen as failure in 1905 since so few Americans even graduated from high school. But the thirst for education has only grown in the intervening decades. Harper's transfer pathway opened a door, however, and a good many ambitious, hard-working Americans willingly took him at his word.

Implications for Today; Institutional Accountability for Tomorrow

If William Rainey Harper were alive today, what might he make of post-secondary education in America? We think it is fair to say that he would be pleased that his advocacy of the research university has reached a cultural zenith in America, unrivaled in productivity and reputation by any other country on Earth.[30]

Harper would also be astonished and pleased with the growth of his "junior" colleges and perhaps gratified to see that so many regular Americans are able to advance themselves academically after high school. Harder to assess would be his views about the degree to which these regular Americans are authentically able to fulfill their dream of earning a baccalaureate degree.

Harper might say that only the most accomplished should be allowed to transfer but might feel troubled that the number is so perilously low, given students' initial educational goals. He might wonder whether the gap between those who wish to transfer and those who succeed has less to do with their intellectual capabilities and more to do with institutional intransigence and bureaucratic barriers, such as the lack of coherent credit-transfer policies.

Or, perhaps, he might argue that the percentage of students who do transfer—overcoming all of the obstacles that stand in their way—are, in fact, the kinds of students we wish to move up in society, having the tenacity, persistence, and intestinal fortitude to achieve their goals.

We might also speculate about Harper's insights, if he were here today, regarding the higher education structure he so richly described as the foundation for the continuing strength of US democracy working only intermittently and only for some students.

But now, with nearly twenty states implementing "free community college" plans and numerous 2020 presidential candidates proposing the cancellation of student load debt, the viability of American higher education is in the spotlight.[31] As we grapple in the new century with questions about the best ways to provide postsecondary education opportunities to the individuals who need it most, Harper's initial vision presents us with three strategies.

Option 1

If the collegiate function of the community college is inadequate or, more charitably, limited in that only a small proportion of students will ever successfully travel the transfer gauntlet, should these institutions narrow their mission to one that does not include transfer?

Perhaps these colleges should turn their attention fully to the function for which their expertise is assumed to be better—namely, training students for sub-baccalaureate degrees and credentials as well as short-term certificates, industry-sponsored training, adult education, and development education. All of these goals are worthy and necessary in a nation that must promote far more individuals into productive jobs and careers. Moreover, they are deeply challenging goals, among the most difficult in postsecondary education.

One could surely make a compelling argument that community colleges devote their limited resources to what early advocates called "terminal education," an outcome that Harper never explicitly defined but could be derived from his perspective that many students would never wish to advance beyond the junior college.

Certainly, these are the kinds of educational goals that Harper might have included in his definition of what constitutes the lower-division and would surely accord with his definition of the community college. Recall Harper's admonition that the work of the freshman and sophomore years represents mere extensions of the high school curriculum.

Modern-day researchers such as James Rosenbaum and his colleagues at Northwestern University believe that, to increase the completion rate of community colleges, these institutions must adopt programs and pathways that are better aligned with the skills of students who enter open-access institutions.[32] We discuss this in greater detail in chapter 3.

Rather than forcing a liberal arts mindset on that work—and its attendant challenges, such as recent controversies over the disparate impact of remedial courses and advanced math requirements—these institutions should view their work as appropriate next steps for high school graduates whose aims are focused on vocational training alone.

Option 2

If, however, we believe that the transfer function ought to remain a necessary part of the community college mission, should it be divorced from all of the other activities of the two-year institution? Certainly, there are models for this. Most large, four-year institutions have separate colleges that address singular disciplinary areas, such as engineering.

Perhaps community colleges could have a "college within a college" by creating transfer tracks that come with specific entry requirements to ensure that students are ready for the rigor of earning a baccalaureate degree. In effect, these institutions would create "university pathways" that would be available not to everyone but only to those so qualified.

Harper had something to say about this even back in 1901. As he argued for restricting the mission of small, four-year, denominational colleges, Harper believed that such institutions could do their best work if they confined their attention to specific disciplines:

> A change in this respect is desirable and inevitable. This change will come partly in the way of establishment of colleges for particular purposes; a college, for example, established principally for the study of science; another college established principally for the study of literature; another for the study principally of historical subjects.[33]

It is not a stretch to extend Harper's notion to colleges that might best address specific academic missions, some vocational, some liberal arts.

Other colleges might continue their training in workforce development but also offer a university track to students who meet specific admission requirements.

For advocates of community colleges who view "open access" as the defining mission of their institutions, implementing admissions requirements would be anathema. Nevertheless, for highly impacted majors such as nursing, community colleges have already put in place course and GPA requirements that are, effectively, not at all different from the kinds of entry requirements that four-year institutions enforce.

In this debate, alas, Harper is not instructive. He never identified "open access" as one of the defining characteristics of the junior college he had in mind. Open admission appears to be a later development that came to define the all-encompassing, democratic spirit of these institutions.

Option 3

A third possibility would be to continue the current structure of community colleges but build curricula within the colleges that successfully link sub-baccalaureate training to readiness for subsequent work toward a four-year degree. For example, could an associate's degree in "engineering technology" serve as preparation for later training as an engineer? Is there any reason that a student who wishes to earn a baccalaureate degree in psychology could not be prepared for this by completing a certificate in child development?

If such linkages could not be adequately accounted for in a two-year associate's degree—it would seem difficult, as an example, for a student learning a trade in welding to be prepared for transfer in English literature—could we serve these students by providing a one-year bridge program that prepares them for this transition to a liberal arts degree at a four-year institution? Or might newer models offering broader on-ramps, scaffolding from certificates to associate's degrees to four-year degrees, become the new standard?

Each of these alternatives could be derived from Harper's original conceptions. Option 1 simply references Harper's notion that junior colleges represent an important extension of high school for many students and an opportunity to learn additional skills that would prepare students for the world of work.

Those community college advocates who would find option 2 objectionable because it undercuts the characteristic of community colleges as fully open-admission institutions might consider for a moment that even Harper believed there was a clear demarcation between the lower- and upper-divisions.

Finally, option 3 merely places community colleges and four-year institutions in the best kind of "cooperative light" that Harper hoped his system of higher education would ultimately achieve.

Harper's legacy is that he left us with a tantalizing but incomplete structure for US higher education—a structure still largely in place today that is, in many respects, a model for the globe. His greatest innovation was the traditional transfer pathway. It is hard to fathom how one of America's reigning elites saw before others the authentically transformative power of higher education as an individual, cultural, and political catalyst, all focused on strengthening a society emergent toward world leadership.

Even if our vision for the success of transfer students and the transfer pathway exceeds in expectation whatever Harper might have believed would be possible in his day and age, he nonetheless lit the fuse that ignited a spark that flickers still. Will it gather to warm us in this new century, or will it finally burn out?

Chapter 3

Second Chances Are Good, But First Chances Are Better

The Role of K–12 in Transfer

"[T]he higher education attainment gap is in fact a preparation gap. For the next decade or more, the battle to make a college education equally attainable must necessarily be waged in the nation's middle and secondary schools."

—Robert Zemsky, *Making Reform Work*[1]

We have devoted significant attention to the inseparable role of four-year institutions in the health of the transfer process. We now reach back to the K–12 sector to delineate the foundational role of middle and high schools in transforming transfer. Unlike other treatments, however, our goal is not to level blame at that segment with the shopworn criticism that if those schools did their jobs more effectively, the disappointing completion rates in higher education would be alleviated.

In fact, our position is that community colleges and other open-access institutions have created special and unacknowledged problems for K–12 at least in direct proportion to whatever failures may be identified in our secondary schools. These stressors create a divide between the two segments that undercut their positive educational intentions for all students.

In this chapter, we examine the advantages and shortcomings of open-access admissions policies—in particular, the hopeful but contradictory foundations upon which these policies are built and the mixed messages they convey to students, especially students in K–12 who may have little understanding of the demands and rigor of postsecondary education.

In their celebration of "second chances," open-access admissions policies deal uncomfortably with notions of academic preparation and the potentially pernicious effect of seeing student's individual effort as the only strategy for

academic success. We offer ways of aligning the work of high schools and
community colleges in ways that support transfer and the completion of the
students' educational goals.

OPEN ADMISSIONS AND THE
CELEBRATION OF SECOND CHANCES

Two characteristic elements have been built into the traditional transfer pathway from a community college to a four-year institution. The first is explicit,
the other implicit. Both are critical to the survival of this important progressive ideal and require the active engagement of K–12 school leaders.

The first and explicit characteristic of transfer is open-access admissions
policies. The community college mission—and the transfer process that represents one element of that mission—allows anyone who can benefit from its
programs and services to enroll in such an institution regardless of their previous educational preparation, financial circumstances, or upbringing.

As we described in chapter 2, the origin story of community colleges and
transfer does not explicitly address the way in which high school students
should prepare for entry to a community college. But the presumption is
clear: high school graduates would have access to these institutions absent
any other requirements of a kind required by more selective institutions. In
fact, many early junior colleges were seen as extensions of the high school
curriculum (in effect, as grades thirteen and fourteen). The transition, however, to a "senior" institution that confers the baccalaureate degree was considered a selective admissions process.

The second characteristic, less transparent but embedded in the psyche of
every authentic transfer advocate, celebrates the ideal of "second chances,"
instilling a message—insofar as our postsecondary education lives are
concerned—that *we* are the narrators of our individual stories and have the
power to alter the arc of our destinies as we wish. Among all of America's
educational institutions, however, community colleges must be seen as the
institutions for which the generosity of spirit embodied in second chances is
most evident.

What other society allows the degree of higher education access that we
have here in the United States via the community college? What other culture
allows its citizens the opportunity to retool, rejuvenate, and rejoin society at
large with new skills and new knowledge—whenever they want and without
reference to past levels of achievement or preparation?

Among all the criticisms of American higher education, the single animating virtue on which everyone seems to agree is that community colleges'
open-access stance is not simply profoundly democratic and appropriately

egalitarian but also economically advantageous for society and the individual. It provides the means of educational ascent for even the most educationally dispossessed. Open admission is the strategy that makes second chances possible, fueling a narrative that drives an individual's notion of upward mobility.

To accommodate these students, community colleges provide a traditional higher education curriculum, helping students who wish to earn a baccalaureate degree with the lower-division preparation they need to transfer to a four-year institution. It is important to stress, however, that typically the largest segment of the curriculum is devoted to many other kinds of courses and educational pathways, some collegiate-level, some pre-collegiate. In fact, five million students nationally are enrolled in courses that grant no credit at all but are offered as part of community colleges' commitment to their surrounding communities.[2]

These courses in totality provide students with training in specific vocations, and develop their skills in writing and mathematics that were not obtained in high school. They train them for industry-specific certificates that lead directly to jobs, provide high school equivalency courses to help students earn their GED, and offer basic literacy programs to individuals for whom English may be a new language.

The curricular diversity provided by community colleges are unsurpassed by any other postsecondary institution in America. For community college advocates, this breadth of offerings is a seminal representation of their commitment to individuals who have no other access to postsecondary education. It also reflects the increasing demand by Americans for educational credentials of almost any kind, regardless of quality, applicability, or, in some cases, cost.

Given the startling diversity of course offerings, it should come as no surprise that student transfer is but one of multiple community college missions. Although community colleges have been criticized for "mission creep," many institutions successfully balance a series of priorities in their effort to serve their students' educational needs.

Still, there are more efficient ways of helping students earn a four-year degree than the vertical transfer pathway between two- and four-year institutions. As we detail in chapter 8, the research is clear that starting at a community college reduces students' chances of earning a baccalaureate degree by as much as 30 percent compared to students who begin at four-year institutions.

The reason, then, to support open access, second chances, and transfer is the best justification for doing what we currently do. Moreover, without open access and the second chance it provides, the transfer ideal—the promise of transformation via individual effort—withers and becomes a mere transactional reality. It is surely true that not every student who attends a community college needs a second chance, but many are getting a new lease on their educational life there.

The Unexamined and the Unacknowledged

Open access and second chances come with an inherent but often unacknowl-edged obligation, however—an implicit *quid pro quo* that stresses the impor-tance of individual tenacity and effort even as it downplays the importance of academic preparation. Part of the appeal of second chances is the narra-tive it inspires: that through the singular investment of energy and ambition, individual potential is limitless, propelling students as far as their academic preparation will allow.

This emphasis on effort is not misplaced. It is powerful and essential. The heroic character of second chances is understood by every successful transfer student as the embodiment of survival and success. If there was ever an edu-cational pathway that reflected and epitomized the energizing effect of effort, it is among students who wish to transfer to earn a four-year degree.

These students understand, even if they would rather not, that the vaguely discernable pathway between many two- and four-year institutions creates opportunities for them to test their mettle, to plan for contingencies, to pre-pare tenaciously, to live with ambiguity, and to develop "work-arounds" in the face of bureaucratic intransigence, lack of on-demand advising, and the burden of deciphering articulation agreements with the skill of a scholar learning a dead language.

Of course, it is easy to be lulled into a certain soft poetry in our celebra-tion of individual initiative. The "Horatio Alger" narrative seems largely unsatisfactory in a nation that possesses an ever-widening economic breach between the rich and poor. Nonetheless, it has proven to be a demonstrably effective transfer student strategy in the US higher education system that is highly decentralized, supporting an idiosyncratic and diverse set of colleges and universities.

Whatever the evident strengths of this system, it is one that inadvertently, but relentlessly, works against students who wish to transfer in the middle of their undergraduate careers. That is why an attribution to individual student instrumentality is essential.

Beyond these general observations, there is a sizeable body of research that supports the power of effort. Five decades ago, psychologists in achieve-ment motivation began to amass considerable data demonstrating that the ways in which individuals explained their successes and failures, especially in academic contexts, elicited powerful emotions that were in turn the source of predictable behaviors.[3] For example, students who explain their test-taking outcomes as the result of their controllable efforts (studying more) are more motivated than students who attribute their success and failure to reasons that they cannot control.

Motivation is hard to muster if your belief-system circuitry is wired in such a way that almost any instrumental action will be insufficient. If you believe you do not have the brains for math, chances are you will be less motivated to prepare for a math test. If you sincerely believe you are a terrible test-taker, it is likely that this will be reflected in your final score. If, however, you attribute success or failure to something that you can control, an attribution that is malleable and responds to your efforts, a very different outcome is predicted. Such a perspective can ward off what psychologists refer to as "learned helplessness"—a condition that represents a profound motivational pathology.

This research has since morphed into more contemporary and sometimes glib notions called "growth mindsets" and "grit."[4] But controlled experiments demonstrate that effort-based attributions provide individuals with the motivation to persevere, to challenge themselves, and to achieve more as compared to individuals without a perception of their centrality in achievement.

Regardless of the framework, and applying a common-sense psychology that has its roots in American pragmatism, the only socially acceptable difference that can be generally agreed upon is the degree to which people are willing to work for whatever they earn or achieve. This does not mean that everyone succeeds. It only implies that the game is not rigged. Indeed, the entire thrust of this book is that community colleges and the transfer process keep the game fair—or should.

But invoking concepts like "effort" and "hard work" as the primary drivers of student achievement moves this chapter into perilous waters, from the pragmatic to the potentially ideological. Agreeable in the abstract, the role of effort is often disputed in our quarrelsome times, especially where educational access is concerned. Of course, there is no level playing field in America. And we acknowledge that effort alone, especially for students from under-resourced groups, is almost always insufficient without supportive educational structures.

There is a trenchant and wholly convincing literature about "blaming the victim" for calamities that are embedded not within individual temperaments, personalities, or worldviews, but in unequal social structures and government policies that make advancement extraordinarily difficult. Although attributions to effort in this context refer only to the internal, intrapsychic causal explanations that individuals use to guide their behavior, we fully appreciate that such attributions can be used against individuals as a "lack of trying" even when no amount of perseverance will suffice.

To attribute success or failure, then, to "effort" can be used to justify all kinds of outcomes, including a rationale for bad social policy or none at all.

(Of course, there are other individuals who argue quite the opposite: that second chances, as financed by the government in the form of financial aid or other strategies, are nothing more than hidden entitlements that incentivize everything other than effort.)

Ideological differences notwithstanding, however, we believe that, without a presumption of focused individual effort on students' part, we lack a starting point to construct effective strategies to increase transfer and completion rates. However, as we discuss extensively in later chapters, we locate the importance of individual effort as part of a constellation of related and supportive structures, understanding that individual initiative, especially for the most challenged students, requires a necessary scaffolding of policies, practices, and resources that serve their tenacious efforts to earn a college credential.

NO PAIN, NO GAIN?

As we celebrate second chances, however, we must ask ourselves whether we have over-played our hand. In our generosity to make college available to *everyone*, have we undermined our ability to serve *anyone*? Despite the lofty and generous intentionality of open-access policies, their presence poses a formidable educational challenge (if not a stark contradiction). Cogent arguments are available stressing that open access community colleges have a negative impact on student degree completion.[5]

Doesn't an individual need to be prepared for college? If we make no provision for academic preparation, are we not staking students' success on the transformative effects of effort as the only driver of achievement—indeed, as the necessary and sufficient strategy of their success in college?

And if a college has no admissions requirements, are we telegraphing to prospective students that working hard in high school to earn a place in higher education is not required? Paradoxically, open-admission policies appear to underestimate the effort needed to gain college entry while seeming to overemphasize the importance of effort once students are enrolled there.

Disengaged and Unprepared

Data indicate that students become increasingly disengaged as they proceed through secondary school. Recent Gallup surveys show 74 percent of fifth-grade students are engaged in their learning, based on self-reported measures of their enthusiasm for school and their level of involvement. But the percentage of engaged students drops to 34 percent by twelfth grade.

More concerning, the percentage of "not engaged" or "actively disengaged" students—26 percent among fifth-graders—jumps to 64 percent by the last year of high school.[6] Not surprisingly, engaged students are far more likely to achieve postsecondary academic success.

Surveys also reveal that a large proportion of high school students who plan to enroll in college do not see a strong link between effort and college-going. Although most high school students expect to attend college, many have no clear idea how to get there.[7] Moreover, many students, both college-bound and non-college-bound, see almost no link between working hard in high school and college success.[8] A Northwestern University study found that:

- Only 28 percent of college-bound students agreed with the following statement: "[High] school teaches me valuable skills."
- Nearly half (44 percent) concurred with this statement: "Even if I do not work hard in high school, I can still make my future come true."
- Forty-one percent agreed with this statement: "People can do OK even if they drop out of high school."[9]

The study's author goes on to point out that the most discouraging aspect of these data is that, in exerting little effort in high school, students believe that their minimal efforts will result in few penalties. Only later, of course, will they realize their mistake, enrolling in college without the requisite skills to match their ambitions. Students beginning college without the skills they need to do college work—even if they manage to stay in college for more than a year—are far less likely to earn any kind of degree.

More than 83 percent of students who earned low grades in high school and who planned to go to college and earn a bachelor's degree fail to do so, and more than 92 percent of students with low grades who planned to go college and earn an associate's degree similarly fail.[10]

Why do some students lack appreciation for the importance of a strong high school foundation for future academic success? One reason might be that they view access to higher education as relatively easy because of the existence of open-access institutions. They may perceive these institutions as an extension of high school and not as a substantive leap from one type of schooling to another.

In a survey of students in six states, a Stanford University study discovered that over 80 percent of prospective college students did not understand preparation requirements for college, and they believed that community colleges had no academic standards.[11] The study's authors also emphasized that most community college–bound students did not understand that they would be unable to do college-level work if their performance in high school had been low.[12]

Running in Place

Since open-access institutions establish no admission requirements, what
is it we are offering to students besides an open door to college, albeit a
gracious and low-cost one? As we celebrate their efforts to earn a college
credential, do we believe it indiscreet to inquire about the completeness
of their intellectual toolkit that will aid them in this journey? Are we concerned that in doing so we will imply that they are unworthy or unready
for this path?

Is it better, then, to presume the best, allowing each student to rise to whatever level his or her current talents will allow? That has been the plan up to
now. Are we satisfied with the outcomes, as measured by students' degree
completion rates?

Many students rise to the challenge we have placed before them in open-
access institutions. It is a demonstrable fact that thousands of students transfer
every year. In fact, transfer advocates—the current authors included—almost
always emphasize that those students do as well as, if not better, compared
to students who began as first-year students at the four-year institution.[13]
But these astonishing students are uncharitably, though perhaps accurately,
viewed as outliers. In *Crossing the Finishing Line*, William Bowen and his
colleagues suggest that:

> "[The] superior graduation rates among transfers . . . reflect strong selection
> effects. That is, students who come to four-year institutions from two-year
> colleges have already successfully managed the transitions from high school
> to one kind of college experience. We strongly suspect that their subsequent
> success at a four-year institution, compared with the outcomes of first-time
> freshmen, reflects differences in aspirations, maturity, social capital, and
> coping.[14]

The efforts of students who "stay the course" are clearly instrumental, but
their efforts form part of a constellation of other helpful factors, some of
which may be out of reach or insufficiently deployed by students from
under-resourced backgrounds. Combing the literature for evidence that
students who start at a community college would not unduly delay their
achievement of a baccalaureate degree compared to students who begin
at four-year institutions, one of the current book's authors concluded (in
frustration):

> Despite 100 years of trying to make transfer work, the unvarnished reality of
> college-going in the United States has yet to be undone: Academically well-
> prepared students who attend community college and transfer to four-year

institutions succeed; marginal students who *can only* attend a community college may not. (author's emphasis)[15]

It appears to us altogether naive to assume that all students will succeed on tenacity and good intentions alone, especially those who have indeterminate collegiate skills. Degree completion rates at open-access institutions bear this out.

Faculty from open-access institutions will surely dispute, as they must, our claim that student effort is the only animating force that propels students educationally. Surely the special qualities of public community colleges support students as they progress toward their educational goals.

Faculty focus on, for example, teaching and pedagogy, as opposed to research, which is routinely invoked as a significant and positive force, is a devotion legitimately lauded by politicians and the public. Moreover, these institutions are characterized by smaller class sizes as compared to the lower-division offerings at large, public, four-year institutions, allowing greater student-teacher interaction.

Finally, it can be argued that geographic access and familiarity, along with low tuition costs (on average), play key roles in advancing the educational success of students who might have no other access to postsecondary education.

We wish no dispute with hard-working and dedicated faculty in open-access institutions. We know all of the aforementioned characteristics to be present throughout community colleges nationally, and we have witnessed the transformative qualities of influential faculty in our own educational lives. There are daily examples of educational victories that result directly from the expertise and dedication of faculty in multiple roles.

We also know that open-access institutions are not sufficiently funded for the mandate they are asked to fulfill. This has resulted in reliance on significant numbers of adjunct faculty members, who have less opportunity to meet and mentor their students.[16] The lack of adequate counseling and advising on two-year campuses is well documented.[17] The inadequacies in US financial support of open-access institutions show up on the ledger in all kinds of ways, from low completion rates to high levels of remediation.

To agree that community colleges and other open-access institutions are special places should not constrain us, however, from a debate around what we really expect from students who begin their postsecondary careers at these institutions. Can faculty and staff be expected to achieve success with all students, particularly those with weak or nonexistent collegiate academic skills?

An argument could be made that whatever criticisms community colleges and other open-access institutions have weathered with regard to low completion rates can be laid at this door of an open-access policy that may predispose students and institutions for greater likelihood of failure. Open access brings with it a series of challenges that appear to be almost insurmountable for community colleges and higher education generally.

We are neither suspicious of nor antithetical to open-access admissions policies. In raising the potentially problematic elements of this generous opportunity—colloquially referred to as "open-door admissions" for a good reason—we remain confident of its future. It is hard for us to conceive of an American higher education system without community colleges or the transfer function that provides postsecondary opportunities heretofore offered only to students attending elite institutions.

Community colleges and other open-access institutions are, for most of the students who enroll there, less destinations of choice than outposts for people who have nowhere else to turn. Community colleges already serve 34 percent of all federal Pell Grant recipients, and they welcome sizeable proportions of students from racial and ethnic backgrounds that have been traditionally underrepresented in higher education. This includes 56 percent of American Indian students currently enrolled in higher education, 52 percent of Hispanic students, 42 percent of African American students, and 39 percent of Asian Americans students.[18]

Some will argue that students attending selective institutions must also prove their mettle; effort is a key motivator for their advancement, as well. In fact, the bet they are making may be riskier, given the greater academic competition they will face. But the cost for students who are from low-income backgrounds or similarly disadvantaged contexts attending nonselective institutions is inherently higher, even perilous.

Often the recipient of insufficient or inadequate academic preparation and possessing fewer resources with which to buttress their postsecondary educational efforts, these students will find that failure of any kind has economic and intrapsychic consequences. They might be saddled with debt and no credential, effectively preventing many from achieving a family-sustaining job.

Moreover, failing in college, especially at a college having no entry requirements, may discourage students from pursuing the kind of lifelong learning that the new century demands. Indeed, the students most likely to suffer the consequences of a poor educational experience are those least able to overcome the effects. Students from educationally disadvantaged backgrounds are less likely to come from college-going families and to possess the related social capital that sustain student academic efforts.

RAPPROCHEMENT AND REALIGNMENT

The collegiate function of the community college is embodied in its commitment to transfer. To sustain this mission, students must possess foundational skills best gained in middle and high school. The record of failure in our ability to remediate skill deficiencies in postsecondary settings is persuasive enough.

It is an unsettling premise that, if you failed to master in high school the skills needed to succeed in college, you are unlikely to master them quickly in a more intensive postsecondary education setting. This is not a call for the elimination of developmental education programs, but is merely an insistence that we elevate first chances as a better strategy.

In what ways should we communicate to high school students, especially those from educationally disadvantaged backgrounds, the knowledge, skills, and motivation they will need to take full advantage of what US community colleges have to offer? If the doors to community colleges are to remain open, we need to meet students on their own terms. But it does not follow that community colleges should ignore the importance of prospective students to demonstrate the skills gained from a high-quality high school education.

Indeed, community colleges may be the institutions that are most influential in demonstrating to students who might not otherwise consider college that working hard in high school has a tangible payoff. These institutions are local, and they are among the most welcoming of all US postsecondary institutions precisely because of these regional roots. These institutions exist to make second chances happen. But embracing first chances is, on balance, the more generous goal.

One of the best ways in which community colleges can encourage greater student effort in high school is to show how courses required in high school develop skills for college-level work. The research from Stanford described earlier reveals that high schools and colleges rarely engage in activities that bridge the curricular divide. This divide frustrates students, families, teachers, and counselors.

The authors recommend that K–12 standards and assessments be closely linked with the standards and assessments of postsecondary-education institutions.[19] Such explicit connections can serve as powerful incentives for students to increase their academic efforts in high school. Moreover, it will serve teachers by providing them with a curricular road map to help their students prepare for college.

A second strategy is for community colleges to stress both access and standards. A policy of open admissions requires community colleges to manage, daily, a critical balancing act. On the one hand, they must be true to their legacy of open access while maintaining academic standards that prepare students to earn a college degree.

On the other hand, community colleges too often fail to stress academic rigor as much as they advertise access. Does this reflect a concern that emphasizing high standards and essential skills will discourage students from attending college? We appreciate that every college must attract students to stay open. But providing access without increasing completion rates is immoral—and expensive.

Part of the current rhetoric around "free college," which emanated initially from within community colleges, reinforces a message to students that access to college comes with almost no strings attached. As critics have noted, there are a great many other expenses that need to be factored into an individual's decision to go to college—costs that are normally not highlighted in announcements about free college initiatives. And almost never discussed are the academic demands that college will place on students, despite the fact that it may be free.

Finally, high schools and community colleges should offer academic "check-ups" to students. The saying "you can only manage what you measure" applies well to high school students. Unless students understand their skill levels relative to collegiate English and mathematics—the coin of the academic realm—they will be unable to reach their postsecondary education goals.

The regular assessment of what students know and what they need to know for college success is essential. But such assessments must be low-stakes and diagnostic, providing students, parents, and teachers with actionable steps that will lead to improved skill levels.

For academically marginal students who do not appreciate the efficacy of working hard in high school, recasting American community colleges and other open-access institutions as accessible but academically compelling will signal the importance of the secondary school curriculum. Despite the fact that community colleges are committed to the success of all students, providing second chances is not without cost. It requires effort.

In chapters 10 and 11, we delineate those additional supports that make individual effort authentically instrumental. Supports like financial aid, academic advising, and childcare are all ways of providing students with the scaffolding that ensures effortful progress. But before any of that can be called a good investment, community colleges and high schools must be fully aligned: although American education will always provide second chances, first chances are almost always better.

Chapter 4

The Rise of Dual Credit

"It is undoubtedly easier to think soundly about a liberal education if you are preparing to give it only to the few who are favored in natural endowments or economic position. But democracy is right and we must solve the problem of giving to everyone the sort of college education that is most readily given to the favored few."

—Mortimer J. Adler, *Reforming Education*[1]

The US educational landscape has become increasingly complex and provides a wider range of student options than ever before. A traditional "transfer student" began at a community college, completed an associate's degree, and then transferred to a four-year institution. This is no longer the typical pathway.

Today's students are now "swirling," attending numerous institutions and frequently combining academic credit from four, five, or more sources into a degree. Many students begin the process of amassing transferrable credit when they are in high school, with courses broadly labeled as "dual credit" or "dual enrollment."

This rise of dual credit both enhances and complicates an already complex landscape for students and families, and it presents new challenges for the institutions they attend. Great variation exists by state with regard to terminology, but these broad types of dual-credit courses earned while still in high school include: Advanced Placement (AP) courses; dual or concurrent courses where high school students take college-level courses taught either by college faculty or by college-approved high school teachers; early college high school programs where the high school partners with a college or university to provide students the opportunity to earn an associate's degree during high school; and International Baccalaureate (IB) programs that grant college credit to students with a high enough score on the final exam. Whether the credit originates from AP courses, dual-enrollment courses, or IB programs, these added credits contribute to an increasingly expansive and complex transfer landscape where the value, positive impact, and importance of the transfer function becomes increasingly clear.

Differences in the ways in which these courses are taught, and in the methods by which students are evaluated, make this educational context even more complex. Some of these classes are taught at the high school; others are taught on the college campus. Instructors of the classes may be college faculty or high school teachers approved by the college.

In some of these types of courses, students need only earn a passing grade in order to receive college credit; for others (such as AP and IB credit), students are required to achieve a particular score on a final exam for the credit to be awarded upon matriculation into college. The two commonalities among all the various types of dual-credit coursework are that the class is presumed to be at the college level and that (at least some of) the students enrolled in the class are simultaneously attempting to complete the requirements for their high school diploma.

What explains this marketplace surge of college-credit offerings for high school students? The demand for these various types of dual-credit courses is fueled by several hopes. In an age that is increasingly focused on postsecondary credentials, dual-credit courses offer early exposure to college-level coursework and are frequently viewed as a means of expanding the diversity of high school curricula while increasing access to higher education.

Dual-credit courses also offer a promising conduit for building a more seamless relationship between high schools and postsecondary institutions, as we elaborated in chapter 3. In addition, students enrolled in dual-credit courses have the advantage of signaling to a potential college that they are "ready" for college-level coursework.

Dual-credit courses possibly ease the transition into college with their assumed higher level of academic rigor. Moreover, credits earned while in high school potentially increase student options while enrolled in college, allowing participation in study abroad, tackling a double major or minor, and/or reducing cost and time-to-degree. For policymakers, lawmakers, students, and their families, dual-credit courses offer tantalizing possibilities for boosting college-going rates while reducing costs for families and taxpayers.

The desire to build an educated workforce via access to discounted degrees is a noble and laudable sentiment. However, the notion of whether college-experience courses should be offered in high schools is not without its detractors. Areas of concern for dual-credit courses generally fall into interconnected realms. There is trepidation around the academic quality of these courses, whether regarding the level of instruction, the level of instructor qualifications, or the general academic rigor.

There is also skepticism around the "environmental authenticity" of college courses being taught in a high school and subsequently not providing an authentic college experience. Perhaps a natural extension of the various academic-quality concerns surrounding dual-credit courses is the fact that the transferability of credit for dual-credit coursework is uneven and frequently institution-specific.

Uneasiness about variability—though not specifically addressed on the part of the institution "receiving" credit—is at least partially ameliorated by the quality control of the AP program's standardized national exam. AP credit is generally accepted across all two- and four-year institutions, save for the most elite colleges (which may refuse to accept AP credit or place a limit on the number of those credits accepted).

The reliable standardization of the culminating exam has certainly contributed to the success of AP so that today AP is the largest source of college credits earned in high school in the United States. Understanding AP, then, provides a powerful window into both the possibilities and the challenges that the program presents.

ADVANCED PLACEMENT CREDIT

Inspired by the possibilities of providing high-achieving students the opportunity to qualify for college credit and potentially place out of lower-level introductory courses, the College Board created the AP program in 1955. AP has evolved into one of the largest, most substantial generator of collegiate transfer credit in the United States. Growth throughout the life of the program has been steady and impressive, and for the academic year 2015–2016, over 2.6 million students completed an AP exam, a dramatic increase of 150 percent from 2003.[2]

The focus of the College Board has shifted in recent years beyond the initial target audience of highly motivated students: currently, it features the laudable goal of increasing access. From nearly the start of the program, the College Board has offered fee waivers in the hopes of increasing access to AP courses, both through the Placement Incentive Program and the US Department of Education's Advanced Placement Test Fee Grant.

This access is vitally important because research has demonstrated that AP participation and performance is correlated with higher college-graduation rates.[3] Most studies find that students who enroll in AP courses and subsequently achieve an AP score of three or higher (on a five-point scale) are more likely to graduate from college, as compared to peers who take the course (but not the exam), though those students merely enrolling in the course and not taking the exam still achieve at higher rates than peers not enrolled in AP courses.

There is strong consensus about AP courses as a valuable contributor to a rigorous high school curriculum, even though significant questions remain about who has the option to participate in this popular program.

AP classes have rapidly expanded across the country. Currently, 71 percent of public high schools across the United States offer some AP courses.[4] AP coursework has traditionally characterized the transcripts of applicants to selective institutions, but for students from low-income and/or traditionally underrepresented communities, AP courses potentially provide the only opportunity to engage with challenging and meaningful coursework.

Furthermore, although the majority of colleges accept AP credit, institutions frequently require a grade of three (or higher) in order to award college-level credit. Therefore, only a subset of students successfully navigate the educational gauntlet by completing the course, taking the exam, and achieving the necessary course grade to receive college credit.

Given this complex AP scenario, it is perhaps not surprising that AP achievement rates vary wildly. For example, however well-intentioned the College Board, recent data indicate that there are important differences in the extent to which students from different underrepresented groups are able to access AP courses and exams.[5]

Although significant gains have been made in the past two decades with regard to the number of students who have access to, and earn a qualifying score on, an AP exam, access to this curricula varies significantly when examined through the filter of racial/ethnic differences, with 55 percent of Asian American, 17 percent of White, 10.5 percent of Hispanic, and 3.1 percent of African American students completing an AP exam.[6]

Data also indicate differences in AP access and exam outcomes along other dimensions. A series of reports from the American Enterprise Institute for Public Policy Research indicate that high school graduates with AP course credit were more likely to have parents with more advanced educations (54 percent of students with AP credit had parents who graduated from college compared to 29 percent of students with AP credit who had parents who did not complete high school).[7]

Additional data shows that students attending suburban high schools have far greater access to AP courses compared to students attending schools in urban and rural areas.[8] Moreover, AP achievement rates are deeply troubling for public high school students who are enrolled in low-income school districts. Data for the 2018 high school class indicate that 30.8 percent of students who took an AP exam were low-income students,[9] but student participation in AP has grown much more slowly for those students compared to students from middle- or high-income districts.[10]

These quantitative measures echo the qualitative concerns of AP course critics. Through the lens of both qualitative and quantitative data, the educational potential and promise of AP courses do not equally benefit all students, and so it raises the question of whether AP courses are deepening, rather than ameliorating, educational inequality. As college professor Erik Gilbert observes in his op-ed for *The Chronicle of Higher Education*:

> How do we level the playing field? The best but politically difficult solution would be to eliminate concurrent enrollment and AP programs. That way, students from across the social and economic spectrum would have the benefit of being in class together, getting a real liberal-arts education. It's worth noting that elite private colleges typically don't accept concurrent classes and are cautious about AP credit. As a result, few of their students avoid general-education courses. Why wouldn't we want that for all students and not just the privileged few?[11]

Gilbert believes, despite the best of intentions, that both concurrent enrollment and AP contribute to reinforcing inequality in the United States. A contrarian might observe that Gilbert's reflections potentially argue that, since the field is uneven, the best solution is to eliminate challenging coursework for everyone.

The College Board has long sought to ameliorate these concerns and strives to create academic opportunities for all high-achieving students by encouraging both access and support for students from all backgrounds to successfully complete AP courses. Supporting this goal are numerous emerging best practices. Inspiring examples of comprehensive student support include AP summer boot camps, extracurricular tutoring, and financial incentives.

Support around AP success sometimes features academic "boot camps" that take place in the summer prior to AP course enrollment and/or provide extracurricular tutoring during regular Saturday study sessions. Camps in high schools across the country—notably at Tabb High School of York County School Division (Virginia), Mitchell High School of Pasco County Schools (Florida), and Pioneer High School in the Woodland Joint Unified School District (California)—have focused on general skills such as critical reading, time management, and organization, and specific academic skills such as AP essay writing.[12]

Generally, these boot camps are offered at no charge to the students, and the camps simultaneously build skills and facilitate the development of a support network with both peers and teachers.

Financial support and incentives aimed at increasing AP course and exam completion have taken a variety of forms. For example, in Arizona's Glendale Union High School, the school district pays for the AP exam for every student that completes an AP course, a powerful investment in support of the district's academic culture.

This financial support "sends an implicit message to students that this is something for them and we believe in [them] so much that we're willing to pay the entrance fee."[13] In addition, AP teachers receive vital, targeted professional development. Trained master teachers are paid to offer mentoring and support, especially with lesson-plan creation.

The Dallas Independent School District, a 2011 AP District of the Year award winner, utilizes a different approach through its AP Incentive Program (APIP).[14] APIP provides tutoring and dedicated preparatory sessions for students in AP classes, with the further incentive that "Students at all Dallas ISD high schools receive $100 for qualifying scores on the exams."[15] Teachers also receive incentives of $100–$500 for every student receiving a passing AP score.[16]

APIP has been notable in increasing the number of minority students earning passing AP exam scores. Prior to the program's inception, in 1995, only twenty-nine Hispanic or African American students earned passing scores on AP exams in the Dallas Independent School District. In 2005, "517 minority students from these two groups received a passing score on an AP exam," a dramatic increase.[17]

Georgia's Fulton County Schools attribute the dramatic increases in the success of their students on AP exams to the summer institute they have created. This institute features professional development for teachers, including a central component whereby veteran AP teachers model effective instruction for new AP teachers.[18]

Other districts have created Vertical Teams, typically from sixth grade to twelfth grade, as a strategy to ensure institutional alignment: longitudinal preparation and coordination across both middle and high school with the goal of helping students to acquire the academic and personal skills necessary for AP success. These Vertical Teams typically include district administrators, principals, curriculum coordinators, and guidance counselors, and such capacity-building programs have made great strides in closing academic achievement gaps in these school districts.[19]

These concerted and intentional efforts develop the nation's potential pool of talent, foster more equitable access to the AP program, and help to ensure the requisite support for student success.

These "best practices" school districts inspiringly demonstrate how we might intentionally utilize AP courses to better serve all US students, especially low-income students and students from traditionally underrepresented communities. Also apparent from these numerous studies is that attempts at providing support for students must include professional development and mentoring for the teachers charged with increasing students' access to and successful completion of AP exams.

The dramatic differences in student achievement when the AP course and exam are provided in the context of access and comprehensive support for both students and teachers raise the question of why we, as a nation, fail to provide both access and comprehensive support for AP in all US schools. To ignore this need for comprehensive support further reinforces intergenerational educational inequality at scale.

CONCURRENT OR DUAL ENROLLMENT AND THE ACCUMULATION OF CREDIT

Although the most common credit transferred into both two- and four-year institutions is AP credit, concurrent or dual enrollment (DE) and early college high school (ECHS) programs are the second greatest sources of transfer credit in the United States. ECHS programs are a relatively recent creation, with Minnesota's 1985 Postsecondary Enrollment Options Act inspiring the subsequent trend of state-level dual-credit legislation.[20] Growth in these types of programs quickly spread, and by the 2010–2011 academic year, an impressive 1,363,500 high school students were enrolled in college courses for credit.[21]

Individual states played a driving role in the rapid rise in ECHS programs, either by mandating that all high schools provide dual credit or by strongly incentivizing them to do so. At the state level, the primary goal generally centered on providing access to a faster, less expensive pathway toward a college certificate or degree. Fueled by this goal, the growth in ECHS programs has been prodigious over the past decade. Based on surveys of high schools, dual-credit enrollments have increased by 75 percent, with over 82 percent of US high schools now offering dual-credit courses.[22]

It should be noted that ECHS can be differentiated from other programs granting college credit to high school students in two ways: first, the student is expected to earn a full associate's degree while in high school; second, these programs are usually located at or near a college campus. ECHS enrolled a modest 80,000 students in 280 programs in 2015–2016,[23] although ECHS has the most potential for longitudinally increasing student educational attainment.

Early research has shown promising results for ECHS programs, specifically for those high school students taking their DE courses on a college campus rather than at the high school. In short, location matters. In the broader category of DE, a Community College Research Center's report reveals that in 2010, fully 15 percent of US community college students were also high school students. Nearly half of US high school DE students went on to a community college after high school, with 46 percent of those students earning a college credential within five years.[24]

In comparison, only 39 percent of students who started community college after high school earned any college degree or certificate after six years (not five), powerful evidence that enrolling in college courses in high school and accumulating college credit significantly improves the pace of progress toward a college credential.[25] Positive effects are also seen for former high school DE students who enroll in four-year institutions, with similar graduation rates of 64 percent but with the benefit of graduating one year sooner than nonparticipants of high school dual credit (in five, rather than six years).

A comprehensive study by Cecilia Speroni compared outcomes for AP versus DE and provides some further discoveries. Her seminal research utilized data from two cohorts of high school students from across the state of Florida, and she subsequently cross-referenced this dataset with National Student Clearinghouse data. To circumvent skewing of the data, the study controlled for the likelihood that AP and DE students were more highly motivated than their peers, and it provides a strong foundation for us to understand how AP and DE programs affect subsequent college outcomes for students.

Speroni finds that "both AP and DE course-taking are significantly related to students' likelihood of college enrollment after high school, enrollment in a four-year institution, and attainment of a Bachelor's degree."[26] DE participation increases the possibility that the student will enroll in college at a higher rate than AP, but DE students are more likely than AP students to enroll in community college (rather than a four-year institution).

Despite this difference in initial destination, the ultimate baccalaureate attainment rate is not statistically significant; however, as Speroni notes, "the effects of DE only applies to students who took courses at the local community college campus, and *there is no effect for students who took DE at the high school*" (italics ours).[27]

Understanding that the setting of a community college campus matters in terms of creating a positive, lasting impact is powerful and salient, and it should guide states as they continue to refine their DE policies. That the location matters, and deeply, is a key point that should guide the creation, development, and refinement of all DE programs.

With this knowledge, states should mandate that DE program courses be offered only on community college or four-year campuses. This more comprehensive ECHS framework would ensure that society's precious investments in education yield the greatest levels of subsequent student achievement.

Another finding from Speroni's study is that the combination of DE and AP offers the greatest potential for fostering student success: "For all outcomes, students who combine both DE and AP courses fare better than those who only participate in one program, suggesting important complementarities between them."[28]

The combination of DE and AP fostering the greatest success is perhaps not surprising when we remember that the completion of rigorous high school coursework is a significant predictor of subsequent collegiate success. The challenge is in replicating and scaling the key aspects of successful high school programming, given that these various research studies powerfully underscore the same central concept: access alone to DE and AP is not nearly enough.

Teachers require additional professional development and training combined with institutional alignment and support, and students require boot camps, tutoring, and both academic and nonacademic support. Sadly, and all too frequently, these costs are viewed as additional expenses that are eliminated when inevitable budget crunches arise. As of 2019, only twenty states offer any financial funding toward their AP programming, to provide either the student or the faculty support required to attain AP course success.[29]

AP and DE programs generate the greatest amount of transfer credit in the United States and thus are essential "home grown" components of America's rapidly growing transfer function. The other significant generator of college credit while in high school is an imported effort with European diplomatic corps origins.

INTERNATIONAL BACCALAUREATE

The IB program enrolls roughly the same number of students as ECHS, with 81,265 US IB diploma candidates in 2016.[30] Unlike ECHS or DE, only high school teachers provide the instruction for the IB curriculum. The IB program is a curriculum imported from Switzerland, where it was originally introduced in Geneva in 1968 as a means of ensuring that elite students (the offspring of the diplomatic corps) were provided a seamless curriculum regardless of parental work-mandated moves around the globe.

Today the IB organization programming reaches students from three years to nineteen years of age in over 150 countries. The program includes six academic subject areas, essays, and independent research projects, along with mandatory participation in a Creativity, Action, and Service program.[31] The amount of college credit awarded varies considerably and is dependent on the state or individual institution's policy on IB credit.

Similar to AP, IB students are required to earn a four or five on the seven-point IB Higher Level exam scale in order to earn college credit. For both AP and IB, no college credit is awarded until college matriculation. The IB curriculum is intended for the final two years of high school, although students are placed in an IB preparatory curriculum on their entry into ninth grade. Teachers undergo extensive training and are required to be IB certified.

In the United States, the program has generally been associated with white, affluent suburban students, but a pilot in a major urban area has shown promising results with low-income, first-generation students from traditionally underrepresented communities. In 1997, the Chicago Public Schools created a set of thirteen IB programs in high schools across the Windy City as a means for establishing attractive, rigorous academic options for high-achieving students in under-resourced communities.

This comprehensive IB classroom effort provided access to cohorts of students (rather than the entire student body) in schools that were approximately 75 percent African American or Latino, and the students were predominantly the first in their families to go to college. A study by the University of Chicago's Consortium on Chicago School Research examined the results of this audacious experiment in their 2012 report *Working to My Potential: The Postsecondary Experiences of CPS Students in the International Baccalaureate Diploma Program.* This was a rigorous mixed-methods study, with controls for prior academic achievement and student self-selection bias, and it found that the IB program "seemed to be taking academically weaker, less advantaged students coming into high school and producing graduates with academic achievement comparable to graduates of selective enrollment schools."[32]

As with AP and DE, graduates of IB programs were more likely to attend and to persist in college. However, these positive results were only for students who completed the entire four years and not for the 38 percent of students who declined to enroll in the actual IB program after the two years of preparatory work. Remarkably, even students who did not earn the IB diploma but still enrolled in the IB curriculum in high school garnered benefits from participating in the program.

If maintained throughout the entire high school experience, the rigorous IB curriculum and environment had remarkable effects. Students were 40 percent more likely to attend a four-year college, 50 percent more likely to attend a selective four-year college, and significantly more likely to persist in college. The study attributed these effects to four key elements: the prescribed, challenging curriculum that runs for all students for all four years of high school; the frequent assessments connected to this curriculum; a strong sense of community and belonging that developed among the students and teachers; and the extensive training that the teachers received from the IB program.[33]

Reception to these persuasive findings led the Chicago Public Schools to expand its IB program, and currently it is the most extensive and largest in the nation. IB has been extended to include elementary and middle schools, and it now includes entire IB schools rather than the original classroom pilot project.

The study drew the attention of researchers from the Johns Hopkins School of Education Institute for Educational Policy who found it remarkable both for its sound research design and methodology and for its strong positive results for some of the most disadvantaged students in the United States. The institute's director and deputy director remarked, "Why haven't urban school districts across the country taken note and, in some cases, at least chosen to build their own system-wide implementations?"[34]

Unfortunately, their colleague and director of the Center for Talented Youth at Johns Hopkins University concluded, "[Those of us who work with] high-ability, low-income students could have predicted that a research study of a program that actually works for them would be of no general interest."[35]

Knowing the positive impact that well-developed, comprehensively implemented programs such as AP, DE, and IB have on students from all strata of society raises an important question about why these initiatives are not more broadly available across the nation. The cumulative refrain from a deeper dive into all of these efforts and avenues that provide transferrable college credit in high school is clear.

There are persuasive, compelling reasons that lead wealthier families and school districts to pursue AP, DE, and IB. The combination of additional teacher training and the offering of a more rigorous high school curriculum clearly fuels the success of US students—but, sadly, not for all of them.

We must challenge ourselves as a country to provide rigorous educational opportunities in every school. Focusing on transfer as having a broader, deeper function than was previously conceived is a central and absolutely vital component of this approach. By intentionally linking US secondary and postsecondary-educational institutions, we build a seamless pool of talent rather than the leaky pipeline of yore.

If every high school student was already on her or his way toward their next educational credential, rather than placed many steps behind the starting line with remedial (non-degree-counting) credits to pay for and earn, how might this transform the educational landscape? If the positive outcomes are so well established, why are we not insisting on transferrable credit being a key outcome of every US high school?

Transfer, long maligned and associated with low income, traditionally underrepresented community college students of a post-traditional age, must be repositioned as the basic educational infrastructure for all. Our nation's success depends on it.

Chapter 5

Prior-Learning Credit

Honoring Transfer Students Who Work for a Living

"Practical know-how . . . is always tied to the experience of a particular
person. It can't be downloaded, it can only be lived."

—Matthew Crawford, *Shop Class as*
Soulcraft: An Inquiry into the Value of Work[1]

Transfer presents tremendous untapped potential to increase degree attainment in the United States by creating linkages within the higher education
system. As the previous chapter demonstrates, research reveals that credit
earned while still in high school—whether from Advanced Placement,
Early College High School, dual enrollment, or International Baccalaureate
programs—contributes to future collegiate success.

This is true whether success is measured in a shorter time-to-degree, higher
persistence, or higher graduation rates. Expanding the transfer function in this
way helps to bridge the secondary and postsecondary sectors for the majority
of US students—not just the privileged few.

As we contemplate the necessity of repairing the linkage between K–12
schools and postsecondary-education institutions, our hard-wiring of academic opportunity for all students must embrace those individuals with
diverse life-trajectories. That includes those whose plans after high school
might not include college but who nonetheless garner experience in the workforce, the military, or their local communities.

Most Americans understand that a highway runs from college to the work
force, but careers may also inspire and lead back to higher education. As the
need for lifelong education becomes increasingly essential for all individuals, the US educational system needs to honor (or at least take account of)

the learning and knowledge attainment that occurs outside of the formal, academic classroom for neo-traditional students.

Perhaps not coincidentally, this is happening at a time in American higher education when the call for student internships and "work-place learning" is increasingly demanded by traditional parents and students alike, because such work is seen as an accelerant into corporate careers.

The powerful, positive results gained from connecting secondary and post-secondary institutions via transfer, as described in the previous chapter, give hope that a broader and bolder pathway that increases intentional connections with military, business, and industry partners can be expanded. This would result in an integrated postsecondary educational highway with multiple on-ramps and off-ramps leading to greater and lifelong educational opportunities for all students.

Transfer credit from noncollegiate sources are an important yet relatively recent addition to the American educational landscape. Understanding the history and types of what has become known as "prior-learning credit" as well as the benefits, impacts, and challenges of this newer source of transfer credit is essential to tapping more deeply into this educational wellspring.

The history of awarding credit for noncollegiate learning began back in the 1940s.[2] Out of the sixteen million returning World War II veterans, many wanted to receive academic credit for what they had learned in the service. Finding a way to apply this prior learning toward an academic degree or certificate would allow the United States to harness its substantial investments in military education and training while encouraging individual secondary-degree attainment.

With this patriotic impetus, the American Council on Education (ACE) launched an initiative that provided credit and transcript recommendations for how colleges and universities might best account for the education and training that returning veterans had received in the military.

Although not itself accredited, ACE's recommendations meant that colleges and universities could, at their own discretion, award academic credit for prior learning earned while in the military. Thus, the earliest acceptance of prior-learning credit was ACE's effort to establish a clear, national process for the awarding of academic credit for military training.

Credit for prior learning (CPL), also known as prior-learning assessments (PLA) and now sometimes simply called learning assessment, powerfully delivers substantial public and private benefits. PLA allowed the nation to reap its educational investments in service men and women while it provided individual veterans with accelerated pathways toward their degrees.

Buoyed by this early success, ACE launched the College Credit Recommendation Service (CREDIT) in 1974, which expanded the awarding of academic credit for appropriate military training into the civilian arena. In a game-changing move, CREDIT added the review of civilian employer-administered training to its review portfolio of courses and certifications offered by the military and other governmental agencies. This shift significantly expanded the awarding of academic credit, subsequently decreasing both the time-to-degree and the cost-per-degree for those awarded prior-learning credit.

The demographics of those seeking prior-learning credit demonstrate that the primary beneficiaries are working adults. In a 2013 ACE survey of those requesting prior-learning credit, 72 percent of the respondents were working full time; the average age was 41 years (75 percent were 32 years or older); and 68 percent identified as White, 13 percent as African American, 9 percent as Hispanic, and 3 percent as Asian American.[3]

Mature, working adults are clearly the beneficiaries of the growing acceptance of ACE's efforts. This is especially notable given that one in five Americans of working age has some college credit but no degree. Compared with the roughly three million traditional first-year college students in America, there are roughly thirty-six million post-traditional-age students with some college credit and no degree.[4]

For these potential students, receiving prior-learning credit is a powerful motivator toward completing a degree more easily and at a lower cost. Assisted by ACE's framework and recommendations, 92 percent of US campuses currently award academic credit for prior learning, and PLA is increasingly viewed as an important vehicle for supporting educational attainment, especially among adult, post-traditional-age students.[5]

Various studies have demonstrated successful outcomes for PLA students in specific institutional contexts, but a recent national study has evidenced dramatic, positive outcomes that hold true across institutional type and size.

The Council for Adult and Experiential Learning (CAEL), with the support of the Lumina Foundation for Education, utilized the records of 62,475 adult students who matriculated in 2001–2002 at forty-eight colleges and universities, both public and private, across all regions of the United States.[6] The research study followed this cohort for seven years, with remarkable results. More than half (56 percent) of the PLA students earned a postsecondary degree within seven years, whereas only 21 percent of the non-PLA students completed a degree.

These positive findings increased by degree level, as students successfully navigated their associate's degree and continued onward to their bachelor's degree. The most dramatic results were for the 45 percent of students who received credit for prior learning and earned a bachelor's degree, compared to only 15 percent of the students without prior-learning credit. Stated another way, students with PLA credit seeking a bachelor's degree were three times as likely to complete their degree compared to similar students without PLA credit.

For those who received an associate's degree, more than twice as many, or 13 percent, of the PLA students received a degree as compared to only 6 percent of the non-PLA students. These are extraordinary outcomes, with aggregate results that are more than two-and-a-half times better for students who received credit for their prior learning when compared to similar students without PLA.

These results held, even after controlling for institutional size and type and for student age, race/ethnicity, and gender, regardless of the student's financial aid status, GPA, or academic ability, that is, whether they required remedial courses or not. PLA students also required a shorter time-to-degree, with the logical finding that the more PLA credit awarded, the more accelerated time-to-degree.

The positive outcomes for PLA students raise interesting questions of self-selection bias on the part of students who are already highly motivated and academically accomplished, and certainly this is not insignificant when contextualizing their success. This "self-selection bias" was noted by PLA administrators at institutions participating in the study, who also remarked that PLA might be "a powerful motivator, as a booster of self-esteem and self-confidence by validating students' existing skills and knowledge."[7]

Despite these successful outcomes, issues remain around PLA, ranging from individuals and/or campuses being unaware of ACE's credit recommendations, nonacceptance of ACE's credit recommendations on the part of individual institutions, and institutions deciding to award credit only for electives rather than for degree requirements. In addition, campus receptivity to prior-learning credit remains highly dependent on the assessment method utilized, and questions around a perceived lack of academic rigor have led to faculty resistance on some campuses.

Concerns around prior-learning credit tend to be mitigated and receptivity heightened when the credit is awarded via exam. Although some institutions offer their own custom exam to verify prior-learning achievement, most credit is awarded through national standardized exams. These include the DANTES Subject Standardized Tests (DSST exams), Excelsior College Exams, and, most commonly, the College Level Examination Program (CLEP).

Administered by the College Board, CLEP is a collection of standardized tests that assess knowledge in thirty-six subject areas. CLEP exams provide a standardized mechanism for the awarding of academic credit earned outside the classroom, whether from the military, homeschooling, volunteer work, or job experience. Similar to AP, in order for academic credit to be awarded, a score above a certain cut-off must be obtained.

The widespread acceptance of both ACE-evaluated military training credit and national exams such as CLEP are reflected in the data: 83 percent of

American institutions currently grant prior-learning credit from these national exams, closely followed by 77 percent for ACE-evaluated military training.[8]

Portfolio evaluation and ACE-evaluated workplace training and development are two additional avenues for obtaining PLA. However, the level of institutional acceptance for these forms of PLA is substantially lower because currently only 26 percent of institutions award academic credit utilizing either of these methods.[9]

Assessing student-created portfolios that describe and document individual work experience and knowledge is an admittedly more subjective process. Perhaps because of the lack of widely agreed-upon standards and guidelines around the awarding of credit via portfolio review, this PLA avenue currently increases skepticism around prior-learning credit. Portfolio assessment is also time-consuming, and awarding PLA through portfolio evaluation requires the institution to build the capacity to do so.

CAEL is striving to address these concerns. It is a strong advocate for supporting, developing, and promoting rigorous best practices around portfolio evaluation, with the aim of increasing its acceptance and use. A central component of CAEL's efforts is the LearningCounts portfolio assessment initiative, which includes an online course.

This self-paced course provides students with guidance and assistance in preparing a successful portfolio with the required breadth, depth, and evidence. LearningCounts also provides institutions access to a network of trained faculty assessors ready to assist institutions as they develop and scale their prior-learning evaluation and assessment efforts.

CAEL's approach toward portfolio development helps to ensure that a consistent, rigorous process is established and followed. The portfolio-assessment method requires documenting the college-level learning that has taken place outside of academia, matching that learning to college-level curricula and competencies, linking the student's prior learning with both career and educational objectives, and demonstrating the mastery of specific competencies with evidence.

As of 2019, institutions generally elect either to outsource the portfolio evaluation to CAEL or to evaluate the portfolios "in-house" with faculty trained as certified portfolio assessors. Some hybrid models are also emerging that blend the offering of a more inexpensive local portfolio-assessment course for students but with the evaluation component externally handled by CAEL.

Because only roughly a quarter of institutions currently accept PLA via portfolio assessment, students tend to respond as one might expect. When considering institutions, they seek colleges and universities that will accept their credits. Currently, the institutions that are more likely to award prior-learning credit tend to be community colleges or proprietary institutions.

Of course, savvy students are figuring out how to create workarounds. As one determined university student noted, "I had to do some advance planning as the ACE units I had received were not accepted by my university. I transferred them to a participating community college and then transferred all credits through the AA degree that the university must accept."[10]

This lack of consistency around credit acceptance creates confusion for students, though it simultaneously increases opportunities for institutions to "game" the system. Because each institution has its own policies (and has the discretion to do so), if a student transfers to a different institution, those credits may be reevaluated by the receiving institution.

Creating a transparent, consistent system around the awarding of PLA would, therefore, help to make these credits more universally accepted. Importantly, the development of a transparent and consistent system would also help to establish campus practices, policies, and procedures that would foster a more receptive campus ecosystem around the students seeking PLA.

This need for consistency around PLA has led some states to implement system-wide standards in the hopes of improving student mobility as they transfer from one institution to another.

Currently there are multiple, relatively new, statewide and multistate efforts to expand PLA. For example, the state of Tennessee was awarded a Complete College America grant with funding from the Bill and Melinda Gates Foundation. A key deliverable of their Complete College America award was the creation of statewide standards regarding PLA. The result was the establishment of a consistent and accessible process for awarding and transferring credits earned through prior learning for the Tennessee Board of Regents and for all public Tennessee universities and community colleges.[11]

This, in turn, put pressure on the private universities and colleges in Tennessee to establish similar PLA policies and procedures, which included valuable recommendations for a maximum of credits earned through PLA, with a maximum of sixty for the bachelor's degree and thirty for the associate's degree. The Tennessee task force also determined that PLA may be broadly applied in a student's program, fulfilling majors, minors, concentrations, and both general education and elective degree requirements. Tennessee's standards were adopted in 2012.

In addition to facilitating the adaptation of PLA standards in Tennessee, CAEL also helped to create PLA policies and procedures in three separate statewide systems: the Montana University System, the Ohio Department of Higher Education, and the Texas A&M University System. These efforts were part of a larger Lumina Foundation–funded *State System PLA Adoption* project.[12] This undertaking focused on enhancing system-wide efforts to advance PLA utilization.

The lessons and recommendations that emerged from these various system-level initiatives provide helpful guidance to any institution or system seeking to expand PLA efforts, whether in terms of timing and sequencing, planning and inventorying, engaging key, or promoting change management around PLA adoption. Most importantly, these system-level efforts underscore the extent to which the US educational landscape is shifting, especially in terms of a growing awareness, acceptance, and adaptation of PLA.

As these transformations continue, whether initiated by individual students, state politicians and legislators, institutions, or state-wide systems, both the challenges and the opportunities will become more pressing. As noted, of the various forms of PLA, the acceptance rates are the highest for the awarding of credit through examination (such as CLEP) or experience gained through the military.

This multi-system Lumina Foundation project underscored that greater challenges exist for the successful adaptation and utilization of portfolio-based assessments, especially around awarding PLA credit for learning obtained via workforce training and development.

The resistance to workplace PLA is as ironic as it is misplaced because it coincides with a rising number of institutions emphasizing experience-based education, community-based scholarship, and the evaluation and awarding of academic credit for unpaid internships. These types of experiential learning are favorably viewed by students and their families because they believe these "real world" experiences will be helpful in securing post-graduation employment.

Although there is increased excitement around the traditional-aged student receiving academic credit for an industry internship, this enthusiasm is strongly tempered (or nonexistent) for the nontraditional, working adult student seeking credit for their prior learning, especially in more elite institutions.

There are now thirty-six million Americans with some college credit and no degree. Rather than seeing these potential students as "nontraditional" or "post-traditional-aged" students, we might better serve our country to recognize that they are now neo-traditional students. Given the US demographic shifts, this is the new normal.

The yawning disconnect between wanting to recognize and transcript internships and community-based learning for traditional-aged students and resisting awarding credit for prior learning from neo-traditional students is a looming social equity and justice issue. Potential "best practices" solutions must work transparently and equitably for both traditional and neo-traditional students to be effective and just.

It is important to acknowledge a general faculty unease with the intersection of the academy and corporate entities. This skepticism adds significant and broad-based challenges around the awarding of academic credit for industry experience and learning. In short, PLA makes many faculty uncomfortable. A 2012 *Inside Higher Ed* comment is indicative of this skepticism: "When done right, the process is a far cry from taking money to offer credit for 'life experience.'"

But that notion persists. And, perhaps more fairly, some in higher education worry that "the 'completion agenda' is putting pressure on colleges to lower the bar for a degree or credential, including through prior learning."[13] Perhaps faculty would be less resistant if they knew that, rather than just "giving away credits," students with PLA take 9.9 more academic course credits than their non-PLA peers with similar profiles.

Although perhaps counterintuitive at first blush, consider the fact that adults with PLA are 2.5 times more likely to achieve their college degree than students without any prior-learning credit. Because they are more likely to persist than their peers without access to PLA, they generate higher numbers of credits as they move toward the completion of their degree.[14] This means that because students with PLA are retained at a higher rate and subsequently re-enroll for the next semester, they generate more credit hours toward their degree.

As the pressure for engaged learning practices increases for traditional students, there is hope that the faculty-led development of rigorous models will provide replicable templates that might be adapted for PLA transcription of neo-traditional students.

Acknowledging faculty skepticism and successfully navigating this complex juncture of PLA with the business and industry sectors is a timely, pressing issue. Translating industry experience and learning into academic knowledge while ensuring the integrity and quality of the academic experience is central to forging a dynamic and compelling pathway and partnership ahead, one that is equitable, rigorous, and transparent.

Added to the social justice issue around establishing a consistent process for the awarding of industry credit is a driving question around the market threat. How vulnerable is higher education to industry taking it over? The higher education sector must proactively collaborate with industry to create a rigorous and widely accepted PLA pathway.

The importance of higher education taking the lead around PLA is underscored when considered in the context of the recent announcements around a handful of "big tech" companies, including Apple and Google. As a consortium, these tech giants announced in 2018 that they will exit our public healthcare system and create an exclusive, private model for their employees. It is assumed that this corporate-created, private model will be superior to the current public healthcare system (and perhaps lead to its reform).

Without leadership, guidance, and partnership from the higher education sector, what will employee educational profiles look like in the future? Like healthcare, will leading corporations eschew higher education degrees in the majority of their potential employees, seeking instead to take care of and train their own and the rest be damned?

This possibility is not easily dismissed. US corporate entities spend tens of billions of dollars on employee development and training. Indeed, the United States collectively spends approximately $772 billion annually on postsecondary-level education and training, with the vast majority of this investment outside of formal educational institutions.[15] Mega-brands outside of higher education are becoming deeply involved in employee development and transforming the ways that employers and students think about learning.

As Daniel Pianko and Carol D'Amico muse, "In the years to come, who will hospitality hiring managers trust to credential students: Cornell University or the Four Seasons? Will it be Google or Penn State that sets the standards that determine who qualifies as a good computer programmer?"[16] In an era when employers are questioning the correlation between a higher education degree and workplace outcomes, this is not a trivial question.

Within this context, might a partnership be forged that benefits all? Great academic institutions bring to the table academic excellence, whereas intentional and thoughtful global industry partnerships bring the possibilities of connections to employers and their brands, as well as access to relevant and timely content. Approaching this partnership holistically could mean a host of benefits, both to traditional students and to neo-traditional students.

Recalling that approximately thirty-six million Americans have some college credit but no degree, there would be a significant societal gain if more colleges and universities became more receptive to recognizing and awarding academic credit for learning that has taken place in the workplace. Colleges and universities have a tremendous amount to gain from these partnerships, both in terms of acting with a sense of social justice and integrity and in terms of powerfully leveraging their future position in an increasingly complex educational landscape.

Within this rugged landscape, both ACE and CAEL have served as important conveners and as respected, national proponents for PLA, and they have signaled the need for big next steps. Both groups advocate that higher education should seek to create more intentional PLA linkages with industry's professional development and training, utilizing their national organizational expertise, imprimatur, and oversight. Unfortunately, some attempts have not been established in partnership with ACE and/or CAEL, and these less rigorous efforts have the potential to damage the credibility of PLA.

For example, a partnership between Walmart and the proprietary American Public University System evaluated experiential learning for one hundred classifications of jobs at the big box retailer but did not include ACE or CAEL in their process. Instead, Walmart and the American Public University

System utilized the expertise of an anonymous third-party evaluator in a manner that drew attention and made even supporters of PLA uncomfortable.

As a former official at the US Department of Education and currently a senior policy analyst at Education Sector noted, "People are going to jump on any abuse and make it seem like the norm instead of an exception."[17] This illustrative misstep stands in contrast to the over 600 corporations, professional associations, labor unions, and government agencies that have successfully utilized ACE's credit-evaluation services.

Various colleges and universities, some nonprofit and some for-profit, have established thriving PLA degree pathways. Numerous proprietary institutions are highly active in this arena, such as Kaplan University and the University of Phoenix. Nonprofits include most of the US community colleges as well as Thomas Edison State College in New Jersey and New York's Excelsior College.

All of these institutions do things differently, and, again, this lack of consistency points to the work that needs to be done to effectively standardize and build acceptance for prior learning. Strategizing how to prioritize and implement progressive and rigorous PLA processes might include a variety of forms and should build on the long track record of successful models.

First, the process around PLA needs to be more consistent, not only from institution to institution and across state systems but nationally. National standards that utilize the expertise and provide the imprimatur of both ACE and CAEL already exist. These models, if more broadly adopted, would facilitate a more consistent transferability of PLA. Since military credit and CLEP exams (and the like) find the highest levels of faculty and institutional acceptance, institutions and systems would be wise to center their initial PLA efforts here.

Statewide systems that have not already done so would be wise to forge system-level agreement informed by ACE recommendations on exam cutoff scores, course equivalencies, and the number of credit hours awarded. This move would help to ensure transferability of PLA credit and improve student mobility across institutional boundaries.

Second, when considering how best to implement academic credit from the military, the federal government should act on the recommendations from Ohio's *PLA with a Purpose: Prior Learning Assessment & Ohio's College Completion Agenda*. The *PLA with a Purpose* initiative calls on the federal government to "build upon the concept of the regionally accredited Community College of the Air Force and establish a single regionally accredited Department of Defense (DoD) community college for all branches of the Armed Forces."[18]

The concept of a military community college is not new, but this bold gesture would be a powerful move toward enhancing the consistent recognition and awarding of postsecondary credit for the knowledge learned from military coursework, training, and experience.

The *PLA with a Purpose* initiative also recommends that the federal financial aid criteria be adjusted, especially those concerning Veterans Affairs Education Benefits. If the regulations were adjusted to create a higher degree of flexibility around the definition and utilization of "satisfactory academic progress," this would help ameliorate financial barriers that many veterans and service members confront in their pursuit of a postsecondary credential or degree.

Third, those engaging with the more complex arena of portfolio-based review should utilize the standards and training of CAEL as well as CAEL's guidelines for statewide PLA initiatives. These comprehensive guidelines address a variety of issues, ranging from the criteria for awarding PLA to articulation for PLA among institutions to the training of faculty assessors and advisors.

Moving to a higher level of acceptance and utilization of portfolio-based assessments will be essential if we as a nation are to fully realize the power of PLA. The need to transcript experience-based learning, internships, and community-based learning will provide a meaningful template that might provide a higher degree of comfort and acceptance for rigorous PLA portfolio assessments that work for both traditional and neo-traditional students.

As these assessments grow in use, potential adjustments of the federal financial aid policies for academic credit from the military might also provide a replicable model for PLA more broadly. Meaningful limits on the number of prior-learning credits should be established, preferably guidelines that mimic the Lumina Foundation system-wide effort recommendations. PLA is a valuable educational on-ramp, not a highway in and of itself.

Fourth, rigorous evaluation and acceptance of corporate sources of prior-learning credit are potentially the most complex tasks, but efforts in this arena are extremely promising in terms of truly improving the educational and career prospects for the nearly thirty-six million Americans with some college and no degree.

Military credit and CLEP exams are widely accepted, and the high regard with which these are held is a precedent that should be carefully expanded to encompass the rigorous evaluation of corporate training. The best practices of ACE credit evaluation and CAEL's training and evaluation around portfolio evaluation of prior learning should be combined.

Fifth, we must link the transfer of valuable workplace development to the academy. An increasing number of institutions are establishing a standardized, rigorous process for evaluating and awarding academic credit for the experiential learning demanded by our traditional students, whether earned through internships or community service.

As this workplace learning becomes standardized for traditional students, social equity will require that these same processes are applied to the benefit of our nation's neo-traditional students. Validated learning should be recognized regardless of where it takes place. Equity should triumph over elitism, and we should demand recognition of workplace learning for all of our students.

Finally, innovative approaches for embracing neo-traditional students are currently the exception rather than the rule for most four-year institutions, though they are the "bread and butter" of many community colleges. Institutions that desire to be truly receptive to the vast market of adult learners must undergo a transformation that echoes the culture shift resulting in the widespread creation of Transfer Student Centers to welcome community college students to four-year campuses in the early 2000s.

By creating a well-structured, comprehensive PLA process, institutions provide students with critical momentum toward their degree and send a powerful signal that this is an institution that values and recognizes the areas where a student has demonstrated mastery. Neo-traditional students should be encouraged to reach higher levels of critical thought through the formal pursuit of an associate's or a bachelor's degree via a streamlined PLA pathway that recognizes and rewards experiential workplace learning, military training, and other avenues of prior learning.

The act of fostering a transfer-student-receptive ecosystem has previously tended to focus on the embrace of community college students and their community college credits,[19] but, deeper into the twenty-first century, our welcoming transfer ecosystem must widen to encompass prior learning from a broader variety of contexts. Necessity and social justice demand that we do so.

Once again, the creation of visible and viable transfer pathways must evolve in order to remain responsive to the shifting needs of today's students. As institutions increase their focus on transcripting experiential learning, community-based learning, and workplace internships, the US educational institutions must harness the vast potential that emerges out of developing industry partnerships that travel in both directions.

A highway runs from higher education into careers, but careers also inspire and lead back into higher education. Until we harness the full potential of this virtuous cycle, higher education will miss the opportunity to creatively lead the ongoing reimagining of the future of learning in the twenty-first century.

Chapter 6

Competency-Based Education

Promises, Potential, and Proof

"We see a relative explosion in competency-based learning models. The approaches being pioneered nationally . . . have taken advantage of the transformative power of technology to develop rigorous, demanding, and learning-focused programs of study unlike what we've seen before. I believe these models will be scaling quickly, and represent a sea change in the way in which postsecondary learning is delivered."

—Jamie Merisotis, *America Needs
Talent: Attracting, Educating and
Deploying the 21st-Century Workforce*[1]

Education visionaries posit a world in which students' intellectual advancement will not be pegged to seat time but rather to an explicit demonstration of their competence, skills, and knowledge at a pace and at a level that works best for each individual. What is the potential of this approach in addressing some of the ongoing problems that have plagued transfer students for decades?

Does it offer a streamlined pathway, allowing them to move seamlessly from institution to institution, gaining needed skills and knowledge along the way? Does their demonstration of academic competence—rigorously defined and fairly assessed—eliminate the age-old problem of aligning course credit from one institution to another in ways that harken more to systems of barter than to twenty-first-century knowledge transmission? Or is this radically different postsecondary-education worldview simply a synthetic shadow of an authentic higher education shrouded in the pleasing terminology of Silicon Valley fast-talk?

Competency-based education (CBE) is a learning approach that focuses on student outcomes and what they learn rather than on the time associated with learning acquisition. CBE developed out of the model of vocational training and apprenticeships. The approach enables students with significant life and work experience to progress more rapidly as they demonstrate mastery of each specific competency, receiving college credit based on their mastery of disaggregated competencies.

There is no single model of CBE, although within a wide range of variation, several CBE tenets hold. The amount of time it takes to learn varies greatly, whereas the material to be learned holds constant. Students move through at their own pace after they have demonstrated mastery of the specific competencies. This pacing flexibility allows students to move on to the next module whenever they are ready, which may lead to a higher and faster rate of degree completion.

Certainly, the flexibility and self-paced nature of CBE are appealing to students, as is reflected in the growth trajectory of CBE programs. "In 2012, there were 20 documented CBE programs in the United States. Today there are more than 500."[2]

CBE and PLA are closely related but should not be confused with one another. They share a similar philosophical approach that values the awarding of academic credit for what a student has learned, regardless of the amount of time (if any) a student has spent in the classroom. There is also a shared sensibility toward assessment that demands clearly articulated and crafted learning outcomes and that measures student learning against pre-determined criteria rather than a subjective process.

As a 2015 publication by the Council for Adult and Experiential Learning states:

> Students are required to prove and demonstrate, through assessment, what they know and can do. When integrated into traditional course-based programs, PLA therefore brings a CBE component to those programs, allowing them to become partly competency-based in the process. [PLA is] a stepping stone from traditional non-CBE programs to CBE, while supporting both traditional degrees and competency-based ones.[3]

In practice, this means that PLA may feed into more traditional, course-based programs and, alternatively, that PLA may feed into a CBE program. These dual pathways create two different hybrid models. In the first model, PLA leads into a more traditional, course-based program. The second more flexible and wholly competency-based model combines an initial prior-learning assessment with completion of the remaining program through a CBE pedagogical approach.

These two pathways create flexibility for students, but they also create confusion and challenges. The same faculty who may feel comfortable awarding prior-learning credit as long as it creates a pathway back into a traditional, course-based program may react very differently if that credit is awarded for a CBE program. The rich variation of different CBE programs also presents enormous assessment challenges in terms of "comparing apples to apples" because the variety of program models creates a substantial research challenge.

To attempt to address some of these concerns and to provide a more standardized framework around CBE, in 1973, the Competency-Based Education Network (C-BEN) was founded. This network includes colleges and universities that are either already offering CBE programs or contemplating whether to offer CBE programs.

By 2017, C-BEN issued a rubric and quality framework for institutions to use in the creation and assessment of their CBE programs.[4] C-BEN currently includes thirty institutions and four public campuses with eighty-two campuses, including the University System of Georgia and the University of Texas System.[5]

No doubt these institutions and large state systems recognize that the educational opportunities for the thirty-six million adults in the United States with some college experience and no credential are at stake. These thirty-six million individuals are defined by the National Student Clearinghouse as potential completers, and, for the roughly one-third of these individuals who have enrolled at more than one place, they are multiple-term enrollees.

The potential flexibility and recognition of prior learning that CBE offers these individuals is exciting and has generated tremendous interest. However, many questions remain, including concerns from faculty about the CBE pedagogical approach and about CBE further reinforcing socioeconomic inequities.

In truth, at this point, the graduation rates for CBE institutions do not fare very well when compared to other four-year public-institution options. Well-known universities that exclusively or primarily award CBE degrees include Southern New Hampshire University, Western Governors University, and the for-profit Capella University. According to the National Center for Educational Statistics, the six-year undergraduate graduation rates for these institutions ranged from 38 percent (Western Governors) to 48 percent (Southern New Hampshire).

Although all institutions evidenced a graduation disparity around socioeconomic status, the greatest gap was found at Capella University, where only 8 percent of the Pell Grant–awardee students graduated within six years, as compared to 33 percent for non-Pell-eligible students.

This statistical evidence of a performance gap around socioeconomic status raises serious questions around whether CBE programs may reinforce, rather than ameliorate, the social and educational inequalities in the United States. A deep and disturbing concern exists that, despite its stated hopes around equality, CBE might further amplify these existing achievement gaps.

A recent report from the Competency Education Research Series directly examines this question. The report cautions institutions considering competency education or those involved in its implementation to be aware of the potential impacts and risks for lower-income students. The report also attempts to raise awareness about how best to attempt to mitigate those risks.

> For at least some lower-income students, without mitigations, a poorly implemented competency education environment may *increase* the effects of their comparative disadvantages in these areas. (italics ours)[6]

Importantly, and helpfully, the report discusses possible mitigation strategies that institutions should consider employing for lower-income students in their CBE programs. These strategies generally revolve around supporting students as they develop their own skills on how to best "learn to learn," with topic areas including organization, planning, and self-regulation. Developing mastery in these key areas is essential, especially if students are going to successfully navigate CBE's unstructured, self-directed approach.

This preliminary CBE research around equity for lower-income students raises significant questions. Before investing further in the growth of CBE programs, lawmakers and education advocates naturally will want to understand more clearly if the CBE model is effective, and whether or not it might inadvertently perpetuate inequalities.

The Lumina Foundation, arguably one of the most highly respected advocates of CBE, hopes CBE "may reduce our nation's toughest inequalities." Even though it is positively predisposed, Lumina thoughtfully reflects on this study's findings around equity:

> CBE programs—especially in the postsecondary context—often presume that learners start out with these competencies. Someone who lacks these baseline proficiencies could struggle to stay and succeed in a CBE program. *The unprepared would likely be those who are already underserved and underrepresented.* (italics ours)[7]

Currently, there is a dearth of rigorous externally validated studies that would provide the evidence more common in other areas of education policy. In their meta-analysis of the existing research, *Innovate and Evaluate: Expanding the Research Base for Competency-Based Education*, co-authors Andrew P. Kelly and Rooney Columbus analyzed the 380 research studies of postsecondary CBE contained in the Department of Education's Education Resources Information database.

While acknowledging the benefits of CBE, including the flexibility of the program, potentially leading to a shorter time-to-degree and thus the possibility of increased affordability, this meta-analysis was highly cautionary in tone. The researchers concluded that, at the current time, the existing research leaves many important questions unanswered. Numerous studies focus on design, structure, assessment, and practice, but there is a dearth of substantive research around CBE students:

> [T]he research on outcomes was limited. Many of these studies looked at students' self-assessments of their own competencies after a competency-based course or program. Few examined outcomes such as retention, graduation, or job-placement rates. Only a handful looked at CBE in comparison to a counterfactual; just 13 compared CBE outcomes to those from traditional programs.[8]

The studies that compared CBE outcomes to those from traditional programs are largely inconclusive, partially owing to the great variety of CBE models being used. This lack of substantive empirical evidence around CBE program outcomes presents an alarmingly incomplete picture, especially in light of both the growth of CBE programs and the growing numbers of students enrolled in them.

In *Measuring Mastery: Best Practices for Assessment in Competency-Based Education*, Katie McClarty and Matthew Gaertner forcefully state, "External-validity evidence is critical to supporting the claims that CBE programs can make about the relationship between their measures of competence and workplace success, and about the comparability of graduates from CBE and non-CBE programs."[9]

As educators, lawmakers, regulators, and educational advocates seek to understand if the CBE model works, and for whom the CBE model works, they will be hard pressed to find the rigorously tested, replicated, and compelling research that we typically look to for answers. Certainly, arguments around the CBE pedagogical approach should be evaluated and grounded in well-designed research studies rather than based in idealized notions or stereotypical conceptualizations.

This research void has compounded pre-existing faculty skepticism around the commodification of higher education certification more generally and of CBE programs more specifically. Arguments against CBE generally cluster around the belief that successful mastery of specific competencies does not begin to represent the fullness of a liberal arts education. Johann N. Neem uses the example of a history major to forcefully argue against CBE:

Even if one could prove that a history major has met a set of competencies—like learning to think historically, write well, and analyze data—that is not enough to earn a history degree, since one of the most important parts of being a history major is learning about different times and places in new ways. . . . Demonstrating competence, therefore, is only *one* of the goals of the history major.[10]

Neem continues his argument, persuasively articulating his belief that the larger goals of higher education must include the mastery of basic competencies as merely one component of being a history major. Neem fervently believes that higher education must expose students to different domains of knowledge and that, over the course of several years, this intellectual journey has a powerful and cumulative effect that helps students to more fully engage and more deeply understand the world in which they live.

This layered degree progression, according to Neem, has the profound effect of developing students as both citizens and human beings. The ease and flexibility of CBE, he argues, do not outweigh what he views as the more profound and substantial benefits of a traditional degree.

Amy Slaton, a professor at Drexel University and a long-time critic of CBE, agrees. Furthermore, she views CBE as increasing class stratification:

It's a red flag to me, the idea that this is going to be more personalized, more flexible, more accountable to the consumer. If you are from a lower socioeconomic status, you have this new option that appears to cost less than a traditional bachelor's degree, but it's not the same product. I see it as a really diminished higher education experience for less money, and yet disguised as this notion of greater access.[11]

The research around PLA is positive, substantial, and compelling, with PLA convincingly leading to increased educational access and success, even when controlling for socioeconomic status. However, the emerging research evaluating CBE is not convincing, at least not at the present time.

Compounding this lack of persuasive research is the fact that the rising number of educational choices now available are increasingly bewildering to prospective students, especially for first-generation, low-income, and/or students from traditionally underrepresented communities.

Weighing the economic costs and benefits of higher education while understanding the relative quality of institutions and programs and the potential value (or lack thereof) to a potential employer is a complicated gauntlet, even for the savviest consumers. Clearly, greater numbers of choices do not equal greater social equality, and this plethora of choices may, in fact, legitimize and perpetuate social inequality.

As a nation, we need to be assured that the architecture of our higher education system is constructed in such a way that it reduces the number of suboptimal choices and encourages students toward their best choices. Certainly, we do not want to add a CBE option into our nation's higher education system if it socially constrains and stratifies, further reinforcing intergenerational poverty and inequality.

As stated, there is no single CBE model. CBE programs exist with tremendous varieties that utilize and combine different models and various approaches. Until the evaluation of CBE moves from anecdotal support to a more positive, nuanced, and contextualized body of research about which forms of CBE work (if any), and with what types of learners, then competency-based education will remain a fascinating yet largely untested pedagogical approach.

Given the current absence of compelling outcomes-focused research at this time, CBE has not yet been proven to be a panacea. The CBE approach, or some aspects of it, may eventually be refined and corroborated with sufficient evidence in a manner that fosters student success rather than exacerbating inequality.

Currently, CBE academic credit provides educational access without sufficiently supporting student success and positive outcomes for all students, especially those from traditionally underrepresented communities.

Chapter 7

Online Learning in the Twenty-First Century

Possibilities and Promises

"First, avoid all actions that are haphazard or purposeless; second, let every action aim solely at the common good."

—Marcus Aurelius (A.D. 121–180)[1]

Online education is on a dynamic growth trajectory in the United States. According to Department of Education data,

> Distance education enrollments increased for the fourteenth straight year, growing faster than they have for the past several years. From 2002 to 2012 both distance and overall enrollments grew annually, but since 2012 distance growth has continued its steady increase in an environment that saw overall enrollments decline for four straight years. . . . The number of distance education students grew 5.6% from Fall 2015 to Fall 2016.[2]

This continual growth in online enrollment, especially in the context of an overall educational-sector contraction, calls for a deeper examination into the current state of affairs for online learning. The dramatic, sustained increase in the amount of online credit being earned by students compels a deeper dive into the impact of "distance education" as it relates to the transfer function.

Understanding the typical online student, what draws him or her to online education, what types of online education are proving more effective for which students, and the resulting influence on the transfer function are some of the most pressing topics of today's transfer educational landscape. Online education presents its own unique opportunities and challenges, and these impacts are amplified when they intersect with transfer.

ONLINE EDUCATION: WHAT IT IS, WHO IS
ENROLLED, AND EMERGING TRENDS

"Distance education" is currently defined (rather quaintly) by the Integrated Postsecondary Education Data System (IPEDS) as "education that uses one or more technologies to deliver instruction to students who are separated from the instructor and to support regular and substantive interaction between the students and the instructor synchronously or asynchronously."

Technologies used for instruction may include the following:

- Internet;
- One-way and two-way transmissions through open broadcasts, closed circuit, cable, microwave, broadband lines, fiber optics, and satellite or wireless communication devices;
- Audio conferencing; and
- Video cassette, DVDs, and CD-ROMs, if the cassette, DVDs, and CD-ROMs are used in a course in conjunction with the technologies listed above.[3]

Currently, one in seven (14 percent) of all college students is enrolled exclusively online, and more than one out of four (28 percent) students are enrolled in one or more online courses.[4] Data-definition inconstancies raise the possibility that these counts are misstated, since many individual institutions report (or do not report) blended or hybrid learning environments in their IPEDs submissions.[5] By 2014, graduate students enrolled exclusively at a distance (733,152) were outpaced three times over by the numbers of undergraduate students (2,125,640).[6]

Although the impression persists that many of the distance-learning enrollments reside in the for-profit sector, private for-profits represent only 15 percent of the undergraduate and 25 percent of the graduate student enrollment in the United States.[7] Indeed, the increased scrutiny of the for-profit distance-learning sector has led to a significant 12 percent drop over two years in for-profit undergraduate enrollment.[8]

It is true that online enrollments vary dramatically by institutional type, with fully 70 percent of all instruction offered by for-profit institutions delivered online. Notably, 41 percent of students from community colleges are heavily enrolled in either partly (6 percent) or fully (35 percent) online courses. For example, California, home of the largest community college system in the nation, has created a state-wide online version of itself.

Given the current scope of online learning in two-year institutions and its likely potential for growth, understanding the impact on transfer students is of vital importance.

Simultaneously, the online industry has been undergoing remarkable consolidation. Ten "mega-universities," including Western Governors University, the University of Phoenix, and Southern New Hampshire University, have been rapidly expanding their footprint in the online arena. Each of these mega-universities, which include both the for-profit and the nonprofit sectors, enrolls over 100,000 students per year, or nearly one in every five online students.[9]

Students are attracted by the educational access afforded via distance learning, especially neo-traditional students who may find it difficult to come to campus because of their employment, the responsibility to care for dependent family members, transportation challenges, and/or deployment or disability. Indeed, roughly thirteen million neo-traditional students are pursuing advanced degrees online.[10]

As a disabled returning-veteran student profiled in 2018 in *The New York Times* stated, "'I knew I didn't want to go back to school in the traditional sense,' said Mr. Hayes, who uses a wheelchair. 'I didn't want to be a distraction in the classroom. I didn't want to have people to have to hold the door open for me, or worry about parking.'"[11] For Mr. Hayes and other neo-traditional students, the convenience and flexibility of distance education are invaluable and provide educational access where it might not otherwise exist.

Online education courses, whether hybrid or completely online, provide educational access and are critical in terms of student retention. Most students do not want to drop out or stop out. As they rise to meet the challenges presented by shifting personal and professional life challenges, moving to an online mode of education offers the possibility of continuing to study without interruption. This shift to online instruction, versus stopping out, is a good move.

Research indicates that when students stop out, this puts them at an increased risk of non-completion.[12] Clearly, the access component of online education should not be understated. Indeed, as discussed more fully below, the promise of educational access is potentially redefining and transformative in terms of the educational opportunities now available to students living in "education deserts," where there are few local options.

Mixed Modalities and Mixed Results

A 2018 Bill and Melinda Gates Foundation–funded study, *Making Digital Learning Work: Success Strategies from Six Leading Universities and Community Colleges*, utilized data from six participating colleges and universities: Arizona State University, the University of Central Florida, Georgia State University, Houston Community College, Kentucky Community and Technical College System, and Rio Salado Community College.

All of the institutions included in the study share a sustained commitment to using online learning to serve large cohorts of diverse, neo-traditional students and comparing their outcomes with students placed in the traditional "face-to-face" classroom setting. The report analyzed fifty empirical research studies published over the past decade and a half, and it concludes that "students performed slightly better in mixed-modality implementations of digital learning than in face-to-face implementations."[13]

These findings raise important questions about how foundations, states, universities, and colleges should be investing their educational resources. If research demonstrates that blended-learning environments consistently foster superior student results, shouldn't colleges and universities commit to offering online learning enhanced with face-to-face interaction? This is an important consideration for state policymakers, institutional leaders, and students.

The question of how students might best access face-to-face interactions with peers, faculty members, and other transformative aspects of the campus experience—and how these types of personal interactions should be intentionally balanced with the convenience of online—is shifting and complex. Educational institutions are devising an array of responses to address this desire for key aspects of mixed-modality distance education.

Data from the Gates-funded study also identified a paradox associated with online learning. Despite the fact that students participating in online courses earned higher retention and graduation rates, they earned lower course grades. The report observed:

[T]wo-year institutions generally registered lower course grades for online learning. Higher-education researchers have observed this phenomenon in the past and refer to it as "the digital learning paradox." Retention rates and graduation rates were often higher for students who took a portion of their course load in digital modalities, but course grades were in some cases lower, and the difference varied by format (such as mixed-modality or fully online) and by quality of online implementation.[14]

Despite the general understanding of online learning as a fixed educational delivery strategy, the modality of its delivery varies significantly and has different impacts on different kinds of students. The effectiveness of these modalities is undergoing significant scrutiny.

Mixed Models, Artificial Intelligence, and Online Education

The operationalization and implementation of "mixed models" has varied considerably. Online providers have responded with a variety of new mix-modality educational combinations. For example, Georgia Tech announced—in its

2018 report "Deliberate Innovation, Lifetime Education"—its intention to create "atrium" storefronts for both current and prospective students in key market geographies.[15]

This planned expansion into dispersed physical presences is poised to meet the rising demand for lifelong learning. Georgia Tech's "flexible learning experiences" include a wide range of offerings from stand-alone courses, certifications, certificates, and micro-credentials to stackable credentials that may be earned as an "end goal" or may lead to degrees, either immediately or when a student decides to continue on her or his educational pathway.

The development of various physical locations also positions Georgia Tech as an appealing option for students seeking face-to-face contact as a supplement to their online educational experience. Potentially, a strong network of geographically dispersed locations would favorably position Georgia Tech with a distinctive point of differentiation in an increasingly competitive online education marketplace.

The creation of dispersed physical locations by Georgia Tech emulates strategies already embraced by Northeastern University, Southern New Hampshire University, and numerous other educational entities. Each of these educational providers is mixing online learning with a network of campus sites that facilitates various face-to-face "value-added" activities, including classroom experiences, meet-ups and study groups, onsite career counseling, networking, and in-person mentoring by peers and instructors. As Sean Gallagher asserts in a 2017 article:

> Over the next decade, growth and competitive success in higher education will not be a function of who is able to offer online programs. Instead, the successful institutions will be those who can symbiotically integrate their place-based educational operations and experiences with software-driven analytics, learning science, and machine learning to create a more personalized experience. A more Amazon-like experience.[16]

Gallagher's reference to software-driven analytics, learning science, and machine learning collectively point toward another key aspect of online learning that continues to grow in importance: the manner in which data are being used now (and in the future) to support student learning and success in an increasingly digital educational world. Successful online learning and strong student retention have always required an institutional commitment to innovative approaches to program and course formats, student engagement, and support services.

As online programs become more sophisticated, student engagement now also includes the deployment of artificial intelligence (AI) to refine and further direct course pacing, content, and review in a manner that adapts to the needs of individual students. The most evolved "intelligent tutoring systems" pinpoint student weaknesses while diagnosing how and why students are making errors and thus transforming the educational experience. These systems adjust the course content and material to adapt to the needs of each individual student.[17]

Advances in AI portend even greater future impacts. Building on the exemplars of today, future online courses will be increasingly responsive to students, flexibly adapting and engaging them in higher education in an even more helpful manner. Furthermore, systemically embedding AI in online courses may mitigate or ameliorate the pervasive negative effects of many of the course offerings that currently exist, especially for students most at risk of course failure or failure to complete a degree.

Indeed, the Gates-funded study mentioned earlier discovered that the application of AI in a Georgia State course dramatically improved outcomes for Pell Grant–eligible students from traditionally underrepresented communities. Nineteen percent of students in those groups received a DFW (D, Failure, or Withdraw) grade in the course version without AI, whereas only 8 percent of students in those groups earned a DFW when the same course was outfitted with AI.[18] With AI, a transformation of the educational experience is under way, and with potentially game-changing results.

Gallagher posits a fascinating vision for the future that advantages institutions embracing an "omni-channel" approach that marries the huge potential of AI in online classes with a globally dispersed network of education storefronts (he refers to these as "offline channels"):

> As student demand continues to grow for experiences that are integrated across offline and online channels, colleges and universities must move beyond a focus on their "online education" strategy—and instead position themselves for a more student-centered, personalized approach that integrates both digital delivery and the richness of in-person experiences.[19]

The benefits of the in-person experience that Gallagher touts were echoed in a *New York Times* editorial by David Brooks, "Students Learn from People They Love: Putting Relationship Quality at the Center of Education." Brooks beautifully articulates the importance of personal relationships and emotional connection in the learning process.

As he ruminates about the research findings on the topic of learning by cognitive scientists such as Antonio Damasio, Brooks summarizes, "[E]motions tell you what to pay attention to, care about and remember. It's hard to work through difficulty if your emotions aren't engaged. Information is plentiful, but motivation is scarce."[20]

Although not specifically mentioned in this article, the ramifications must be even greater for students who are first-generation, have low socioeconomic status, and/or are from traditionally underrepresented communities. Life stresses combined with the systemic inequality of under-resourced schools present substantial obstacles—which perhaps only the powerful (and costly) combination of AI and human connection might mitigate.

Deploying the benefits of AI for individualized student tutoring and reinforcing this technological power with human advising relationships might prove to be a promising "high tech, high touch" benefit of hybrid models of education.

POWERFUL INTERSECTIONS: MEGA-UNIVERSITY ONLINE EDUCATION, CORPORATE TAX BREAKS, AND CORPORATE CREDENTIALING

How this mix of AI-enhanced online instruction is best married with "offline channel" campus storefronts will be fascinating to watch in the years to come. It is intriguing to compare Gallagher's "winner take all" approach, which favors both mega-universities and some elites (such as Georgia Tech and Northeastern), with the reality that traditionally most community college students still favor "close, cheap, and easy."

Interestingly, geographical proximity remains important for online students, with over 75 percent of students engaged in online education enrolled in an institution within 100 miles of their home.[21] However, the question of whether the lure of geographical proximity will continue to drive student choice is debatable, especially in the context of the rise of nonprofit mega-universities.

These universities, typified by Southern New Hampshire University (SNHU), have enormous online footprints and impressive data-driven marketing efforts with substantial budgets to match. SNHU combines these particular forms of deep resource investment with a content-delivery model that is highly dependent on adjunct instructors utilizing standardized curriculums and/or competency-based education models.

This should be of interest to every taxpayer, because SNHU relies heavily on federal funds to support its bottom line. For example, nearly half of SNHU students are Pell Grant recipients, and more than 15 percent have ties to the military.[22] While avoiding an exact figure, President Paul LeBlanc of SNHU admits profit margins are "quite healthy," and analysts place their online operation profit margins at a brawny 40–50 percent.[23]

Although they receive a substantial percentage of federal education dollars, many of these mega-universities also depend on corporate partnerships to assist with growing the bottom line. These corporate agreements help tremendously in terms of student recruitment. Arizona State University (ASU), for example, has established partnerships with Starbucks, Papa John's, and Uber that provide eligible employee-students with fully funded tuition for its online programs.[24]

These corporate partnerships are incredibly positive for both partners, because they provide recruitment and retention benefits to the employer seeking to attract and retain employees while they lower the cost of student acquisition for the mega-university. This employee benefit is largely paid for not by the individual or by the corporate sponsor but, again, by the American taxpayer in two forms.

First, students are required to submit an application for federal financial aid in order to receive any employee benefit from the company. Typically, only after federal financial-aid dollars have been awarded does the company fund the remaining costs, colloquially known as "last dollar scholar" funding. In a more submerged (and less discussed) manner, the American taxpayer further subsidizes employer corporate tuition assistance programs via Section 127 of the US tax code. This portion of the code permits corporate tax write-offs for tuition costs as employee professional development expenses at the rate of up to $5,250 per employee per year, to the tune of nearly $18 billion dollars in 2019 and growing.[25]

The benefits, both direct and indirect, to companies like Starbucks are clear. Starbuck's partnership with ASU online programs are beneficial to the company because they encourage employee retention, improve employee morale, and hold the positive potential outcome of the development of future Starbucks managers and executives. ASU-like partnerships are also terrific public relations coups.

Best of all, the cost to Starbucks (or other corporate entities) is effectively nominal, especially when factoring in the "last dollar scholar" funding mechanism that further supplements federal student aid with the federal tax code reimbursements for any remaining employee-development expenses. When considering the average yearly salary of a Starbuck's barista, employee tuition assistance programs are a powerful way to reverse the national trend toward inequitable investments in low-income students and, as such, should be commended.

However, many higher education specialists take issue with the current tax code, and they especially criticize the federal government for providing additional educational funding through the "submerged" mechanism of corporate tax breaks rather than via direct assistance to students or to the academic institutions they attend. Whether or not this is the optimal solution is a complicated question to address.

The Section 127 funding model as it currently stands underscores the broad relevancy of many of the questions raised in the earlier discussion of PLA. As neo-traditional students seek the awarding of academic credit for their work experience, questions are again raised around the relationship of higher education to corporations.

What types of partnerships could or should be possible between higher education institutions and corporations, and how should federal or state policies incentivize or de-incentivize such partnerships? Clearly, articulating the ideal balance and pathways between and among educational experiences and corporate professional development training will become increasingly important in the years to come.

Higher education leaders, not surprisingly, want to be reassured that educational rigor and integrity will remain central, that faculty will guide the quality and content of higher education, and that institutional excellence will be ensured by appropriate accrediting bodies.

Alongside this desire for a high-quality educational experience, higher education professionals remain cognizant of the desire of students and their families for mapping educational pathways into careers. How best to balance this market demand for clear career paths with the importance of the complex learning, reflection, and critical thinking espoused in liberal arts studies is a question that has become increasingly pressing in the neo-liberal climate of the twenty-first century.

One important player navigating this market in the corporate certification arena is Coursera. Coursera has undertaken an impressive expansion of full-degree programs with institutional partners such as the University of London and the University of Illinois. Coursera's substantial revenue growth from digital badges is even more fascinating. As noted in a provocative *Forbes* article entitled "This Company Could Be Your Next Teacher: Coursera Plots a Massive Future for Online Education":

> In an effort to increase adoption of its products, IBM is pushing to train developers, administrators and customer service workers in IBM technology. Coursera charges $39 to $49 a month for these courses, which take three to six weeks to complete. Graduates get certificates and IBM digital badges that can help them land jobs at IBM or at IBM client companies like Wells Fargo and Exxon Mobil. Corporate courses can be especially lucrative for Coursera, which in some cases keeps 100% tuition revenue.[26]

Online Transfer Credit: Reinforcing or Ameliorating Educational Inequality?

Whether from Coursera or other providers, online corporate credentialing in the form of badges is a powerful force with enormous potential impacts on higher education. Online badges, perhaps stacked to form a certificate or degree program, are of particular interest to US community colleges.

Community college students are the most likely to be initially affected by corporate credentialing, simply because they are more likely to be enrolled in online education. Just under 31 percent of community college students are enrolled in at least one online course, as compared to 29 percent of undergraduates at four-year public institutions and only 25.6 percent at four-year private colleges.

The students at for-profit institutions, of course, dwarf these percentages; fully 57.7 percent were enrolled at least partially online.[27] Regardless of their popularity, online courses make the realm of transfer fraught with challenges.

Today's transfer agreements, as they relate to online education, frequently exacerbate existing divides. As discussed earlier, many four-year campuses—especially the more prestigious and exclusive institutions—are predisposed to dismiss courses completed at community colleges as "not rigorous enough." The stakes become even higher around online education and frequently translate into the four-year institution's outright refusal to accept courses completed online for transfer credit, save perhaps for elective credits that do not directly apply to a student's degree program.

Faculty trepidation for any credit transferred into the institution typically centers on questions concerning academic rigor. With online courses from community colleges, these concerns further extend into academic integrity, especially as it relates to online exam proctoring and verified student identification. The academy's frequent lack of clear policies around online transfer credit raises questions and concerns that disproportionately penalize community college students.

As noted earlier, two-year institutions were early adopters of online education, and, as a sector, they have been much more likely to embrace the intrinsic value and the increased educational access made possible by online offerings. Community colleges have adapted to the negative perceptions toward online education with responses aimed at protecting their students, including an outright refusal to note on a student's transcript the modality of instruction for a particular course.

Rather than placing community colleges in the position of resorting to the subterfuge of refusing to identify the modality of instruction, the United States and its educational policies and investments should more effectively utilize the potential power of online education. Yet again, the fundamental threat for higher education is the risk of minimizing its role as the primary provider of postsecondary education.

The submerged corporate tax breaks to mega-universities discussed earlier, the growth of online corporate-generated (and delivered) education, and the fundamental bias against online education combine to raise provocative questions. Higher education should not be sidelined in these discussions. We must take a more active and engaged role, especially if we are to continue to transform higher education for every American.

We should collectively be striving to ameliorate the deleterious effects of what are known as "education deserts." These deserts are largely found in rural areas, where college opportunities are available only after traveling substantial distances. Many communities across the United States are unequal in the numbers or accessibility of institutions in close proximity (generally defined as within sixty miles). A parallel may be drawn to "food deserts":

> Food deserts do not occur at random but are systematically drawn along lines of race and class where low-income neighborhoods and communities of color tend to have the poorest access to affordable and nutritious food, resulting in poor health conditions . . . geography can be destiny when opportunities are richly available for some and rare or even nonexistent for others.[28]

The systematic inequalities built into the current US postsecondary-educational system disproportionately affect neo-traditional students, who generally make educational choices informed by proximity to work and home. These constrained educational environments are in the regions that could be positively impacted by thoughtful changes to Title III of the Higher Education Act.

Adjustments could be made to incentivize institutions to create capacity and better serve students where educational options are the most constricted. Utilizing the best of what we currently know about online education, these shifts could be framed to promote a hybrid model of education that weaves together the flexibility and AI-enhanced capability of online education with the benefits of regional or "offline channel" educational centers.

As a further refinement, states could strengthen academic partnerships among community colleges, four-year institutions, and local businesses so that approved companies serve as "offline channel" education centers, thus building cross-sector capacity in a manner that serves students and responds to local needs. It would also ensure direct and substantive investment in both students and their institutions, targeted to geographical areas of greatest need.

In effect, PLA could "work both ways," with the workplace serving as both launchpad and connective tissue for students and employees. The potential benefits of online education, especially when supported by face-to-face learning opportunities, leverage our nation's investments in our community colleges with exciting and enormous possibilities.

Key updates to Title III might significantly move the dial in terms of increasing educational access and success for students affected by the systematic inequality of our nation's most persistent "education deserts."

These investments must be mindful not only of the promise but also of the current limits of online education for our most vulnerable students. Building these types of cross-sector partnerships might be the most promising avenue to deliver face-to-face learning opportunities that supplement and support online education.

Employers and Online Educational Outcomes

These dynamic partnerships might also modulate conversations surrounding the marketplace values and career outcomes of online students and the current perceptions of online education. In their study "The Market Value of Online Degrees as a Credible Credential," Calvin Fogle and Devonda Elliott confirmed that "employers perceived a traditional or hybrid modality more credible than a purely online modality across multiple industries," though this finding was attenuated for hiring managers who have experienced online education.[29]

Their study reinforced the findings of previous research that underscore employer concerns around the academic rigor of online degrees: "[N]egative employer perceptions . . . include the perception that online students are less skilled socially and by the nature of online education as an individual pursuit, perhaps not as well suited to becoming members of a team of employees as an on-campus student."[30]

With government incentivization via Title III funding, the creation of cross-sector partnerships could simultaneously address these negative employer perceptions and the structural inequality of "education deserts." The intentional interconnection of online education and "offline locations" in both community colleges and local businesses would help to deliver the transformative power of education to all Americans, both urban and rural. Ben Myers's compelling 2018 article underscores this potential impact:

> Americans living in rural areas have been left behind in income, assets, and health. They're also more likely to live in an education desert. Whether it's correlation or causation, a college education is linked to higher earnings, better employment rates, and overall well-being.[31]

Intentional efforts around addressing the educational vacuums found across America would also prove a powerful balm for addressing intergenerational inequality. For example, although the vast majority of Americans living in education deserts are white, the forced migration of American Indians has left many of them in areas far removed from population centers and their educational options.

Almost 30 percent of American Indians live more than sixty miles from a college, and American Indians are five times as likely as White Americans to live in an education desert.[32] In other words, incentivizing the creation of hybrid higher education learning opportunities in education deserts would help to address some of the most intransigent, profound aspects of systemic inequality in the United States.

SUMMARY

The current US tax code plainly facilitates and encourages corporate/educational partnerships such as the ASU/Starbucks model. Furthermore, the tax code reinforces a sobering reality.

If higher education is not a proactive, persuasive player in these partnerships, it will be left behind. Higher education takes on a significant risk by abdicating our role as the direct recipient of public investment in higher education as a public good for all US citizens regardless of where they live.

Instead, we have reached a tacit agreement that ensures a diversion of our limited educational funding streams to corporate partners, with the resulting tuition dollars largely flowing to select mega-universities. Combined with the growing impacts of PLA, a substantial and fundamental threat for higher education is the risk of minimizing its role as the primary provider of post-secondary education.

Situated in this landscape, online education holds tremendous promise for positively transforming our educational system while informing and shaping the ties between the academy and the workplace. With the expansion of corporate credentialing, higher education is at risk of being bypassed at a juncture when its noblest reasons for existence are most central to the conversation.

Online education skeptics should be questioning their own biases. Rather than seeking to minimize or discriminate against the transfer or acceptance of online courses, credentials, and degrees, cynics should be identifying ways to ensure the highest quality with the most equitable impact for all learners. It is not an exaggeration to assert that the US higher education system depends on it.

Chapter 8

The Shifting Higher Education Landscape

"While some differentiation between two- and four-year institutions is appropriate, a rigid, two-tier system, which offers little fluidity between levels, and tends to educate different income and racial and ethnic groups in different settings, is neither inevitable nor desirable, nor, the evidence suggests, particularly efficient."

—The Century Foundation, *Bridging the Higher Education Divide*[1]

The Great Recession in 2008–09 may be the seminal event that historians refer to when they evaluate significant changes to American higher education. Although its impact was felt across the nation and affected virtually every sector of the US economy, the recession's blow was especially problematic for higher education.

At precisely the moment when one of the largest high school graduating classes readied themselves for college, those students and their families were faced, in the hardest hit areas, with restricted enrollments and higher tuition prices. Harvard professor Bridget Terry Long summarizes that difficult time:

The Great Recession has far-reaching effects on both the supply and demand sides of higher education. On the supply side, postsecondary institutions experienced cuts to multiple revenue sources. . . . The level of government support was also impacted, especially in the form of state appropriations, which affect tuition prices. In terms of families, or the demand side of higher education, the downturn of the economy affected incomes and unemployment rates, thereby reducing economic well-being and stability. Moreover, home ownership and home equity levels have declined, reducing a major source of wealth and capital for many families.[2]

Long goes on to describe the complicated effects of the recession on college-going, highlighting a series of leading indicators that affect higher education today. For example, college enrollment actually increased during and after the recession. As noted, part of this was due to the fact that 2009–10 saw one of the largest high school graduating classes in American history. But the character and intensity of this enrollment was different.

Although students entering baccalaureate-granting institutions increased slightly, a bigger boost was seen in two-year associate's degree programs and certificates. Moreover, part-time student enrollments grew significantly as compared to full-time enrollment.[3] In other recessionary cycles, growth is often observed in community colleges as individuals of all ages seek new skills or training to bolster themselves economically. What seems different here is that, in the midst of a large high school graduating class, four-year colleges and universities saw only limited growth.

Enrollment trends are only one measure of changing attitudes regarding higher education, and, during an unprecedented economic meltdown, drawing long-term conclusions is a risky game. Still, whatever else this economic downturn caused, it continues to generate a debate in America about the value of higher education, with "value" often defined in its narrowest sense: a purely economic equation that links degrees to vocational certainty after graduation.

The lingering aftermath of the Great Recession, however, also set the stage for the creation or enhancement of new models for accessing and earning postsecondary credentials, as we described in chapters 4, 5, 6, and 7. These models, made manifest by the development of extraordinarily robust Internet platforms, have the potential to democratize higher education in ways that will advance the education of many more Americans, not only those with the wherewithal to pay for it.

In the midst of this dynamic postsecondary-education landscape, a key outcome may be a broader definition and acceptance of transfer. Indeed, it may be the singular mechanism that characterizes the experience of most Americans who seek a college credential. In this chapter, we evaluate the future of the transfer process in this new higher education landscape.

THE EVERGREEN DEBATE ABOUT THE VALUE OF HIGHER EDUCATION

This debate about the value of higher education is, of course, not new. Historically, most Americans have never been comfortable with the intellectualism that higher education institutions supposedly represent, especially well-established citadels like Harvard, Princeton, and Berkeley. We seem to prefer the practical and useful aspects of our postsecondary-education efforts, always slightly embarrassed to admit that we plan to study something "for learning's sake."

Over a half-century ago, historian Richard Hofstadter warned of the nation's growing disdain for the academic elements of education in his book *Anti-intellectualism in American Life*, and he concluded (in a description that sounds astonishingly contemporary):

> [T]he schools of the country seem to be dominated by athletics, commercialism, and the standards of the mass media, and these extend upwards to a system of higher education whose worst failings were underlined by the bold president of the University of Oklahoma, who hoped to develop a university of which the football team could be proud. Certainly some ultimate educational values seem forever to be eluding the Americans. At great effort and expense they send an extraordinary proportion of their young to colleges and universities; but their young, when they get there, do not care even to *read*. (author's emphasis)[4]

The Great Recession built on this awkward and largely unspoken ambivalence in very explicit ways. It did not simply change the way in which we evaluate the value of higher education. It accosted our conceptions about the legitimacy of the time we spend there and, most critically, what we are likely *to lose* economically by spending four or more years away from the working world.

Whether or not the current rhetoric about the relevance of a traditional four-year degree represents a predictable pendulum swing from the post-millennial exuberance of a surging American economy to one chastened and pessimistic about America's economic future, the lingering result of the 2008–09 crash continues to influence the ways in which Americans view higher education.

Current hand-wringing notwithstanding, the documented effects of the Great Recession are now part of the public record. When its costs were finally tallied, state governments—the primary purveyors of operating revenue to public colleges and universities—had much less money to spend on these institutions.

Private colleges and universities, large and small alike, saw the value of their endowments and other investments sink along with the stock market. Of course, this is characteristic of economic downturns, regardless of severity. Yet the reckoning in this case was altogether different, revealing fissures in the way higher education institutions supported themselves and in the very value they proposed to prospective students.

Of course, state governments were burdened by other public-funding commitments and had fewer resources to allocate to higher education. Analysts point to America's aging population as one reason why political leaders direct less money to higher education.[5] One report finds that increased allocations to Medicaid is the largest contributor to a decline in public higher education spending at the state and local levels.[6]

But beyond the normal political trade-offs inherent in democratic decision-making, the ground upon which the higher education edifice had been built appeared to totter. The recession put in bold relief a general disaffection with higher education or at least a greater willingness to debate its fundamental foundations and theories of action.

Moreover, the concern is bipartisan in a most partisan epoch. Republican and Democratic presidential administrations may differ in their political motivations, but both parties have called for improvements in a system they believe is not accountable to the demands of the US economy. In a 2018 Pew Research Center survey, a majority of Republicans and Democrats (73 percent and 58 percent, respectively) indicated that "Students are not getting the skills they need to succeed in the workplace."[7]

More generally, the public seems bewildered by a traditional higher education system that appears to be out-of-step with what they see as alarming global competition for jobs and opportunity. They would not be wrong in this fear, as some US companies continue to offshore jobs, especially in manufacturing, to places that have no whiff of minimum-wage restrictions.

Higher education must also carry some burden for the public's alarm and concern. There are at least two reasons. The first is a steady but inexorable increase in the cost of higher education. According to the College Board's *Trends in College Pricing 2018*:

> In the public two-year and private nonprofit sectors, published prices are more than twice as high in 2018–19 as they were in 1988–89. The average in-state tuition and fee price in the public four-year sector is about three times as high in inflation-adjusted dollars as it was in 1988–90.[8]

The College Board also reports that, during this same period, median family income was only 18 percent higher in 2017 than in 1987.[9] The gap between the cost of college and families' ability to pay for it must surely be seen as a contributor to the current debate about the value of a higher education degree.

The second reason is a perplexing stagnation in college completion rates. Although an increasing number of students attend college, the gap between those who begin and those who complete a degree remains large:

> During the past half century, the United States has made tremendous progress in increasing access to postsecondary education. From 1960 to 2016, the

percentage of recent high school graduates who went on to higher education increased from 45.1 percent to 69.8 percent. . . . [R]esearch suggests that about only half of students enrolled at four-year colleges and universities graduate within 150 percent of the expected completion time, and the completion rate is even lower for students enrolled at two-year colleges.[10]

One might have assumed that increases in price might be accompanied by an increase in graduation rates. But the two metrics appear to be unrelated—at least to the public and to politicians, giving them license to question the very purpose and promise of higher education. Higher tuition and lengthening time-to-degree rates are alarming to the public and pundits alike. With a government perceived to be in extreme financial distress and with higher education costs rising, families have been asked to bear a greater portion of the financial burden.

Although families had always expected to pay part of the cost of their sons' and daughters' college education, their share has quickly become primary. The average amount of a Pell Grant, historically the federal government's strategy to boost access to higher education for low-income families, stagnated in relation to rising tuition costs, placing more emphasis on higher education loans as the mechanism by which families would support a postsecondary-degree commitment.[11]

The latest data indicate that Americans have accumulated $1.5 trillion in student loan debt, a startling figure that, more than any other statistic, signals both the concern of families about the cost of college and the steady disinvestment of government in a higher education system that it sees as a private good rather than a public necessity.[12]

DEGREES TO FALL BACK ON

A more expensive higher education environment has had a discernable impact on families and governments alike. Families, now paying more, want a more certain return on their investment from the credentials their sons and daughters earn in college. This, of course, is not new. As noted earlier, many families in the United States, even those who enthusiastically send their children to college, are suspicious of degrees that do not appear to offer gainful employment after graduation.

In the past, however, this inchoate but passionate desire to link a college degree with an explicit vocational payoff was perhaps rooted less on disaffection with college itself. If there was uncertainty about the value of college, it was not represented in college attendance. In fact, there was considerable concern, before the Great Recession, about the danger of subsequent generations not earning a college degree. A College Board report released in 2008 concluded, perhaps with some alarm, that:

> As an aging and highly educated workforce retires, for the first time in the history of our country we face the prospect that the educational level of one generation of Americans will not exceed, will not equal, perhaps will not even approach, the level of its parents.[13]

Today, given the increased cost of college and the degree to which students find themselves in debt from student loans, the stakes are much higher. It has shifted the ground on which students base their future. As Andrew Del Banco notes in *College: What It Was, Is, and Should Be:*

> [T]here is a sense of drift. Before the financial crash, students were fleeing from "useless" subjects such as literature or the arts and flocking into "marketable" subjects such as economics. Now, in the lingering aftermath of the global financial crisis, the flight continues; many students are wondering what, in fact, is useful for what. Even at elite institutions, one feels more than a hint of panic about post-college life. Young people know that time-tested assumptions about the best route to this or that vocation, about how to find a mate and satisfying work, how to prosper and save, how to balance needs with wants—in short, how to make a life—are being called into radical doubt.[14]

This radical questioning has had an impact on the majors that students choose. It has also led them to question the very point of attending college. Every generation in youth has concerned itself with how best to make a life. What seems different now, as Del Banco notes, is that students consider less what might be of interest to them and focus more on their prospects for future employment. Additional documentation comes from the Higher Education Research Institute at the University of California, Los Angeles, which regularly surveys incoming college students about their motivations for attending college.

Although "getting a good job" has always been an important reason to attend college, this response has never been higher since 2008. In 2016, about 85 percent of those surveyed mentioned this as one of the primary reasons for attending college. In fairness to incoming college students, about seven in ten say that "getting an education" was also an important reason for going to college.[15]

Although this questioning might be seen as alarming by those of us who advocate for the transformative qualities of higher education, it has benefits, too. Mindful of the costs and increasingly skeptical of traditional liberal arts degrees that (we are assured by critics) offer no direct link to anything remotely familiar to a job, families and prospective students today are more willing to consider new postsecondary pathways and nontraditional degrees and certificates.

As noted in chapter 7, the rise of online education has provided students of all ages with a substantial set of new and innovative choices in what they wish to learn and how they wish to learn it. As we note, these online offerings come with advantages and disadvantages, but it seems very unlikely that higher education will not be influenced by a global Internet ecosphere that has transformed other industries and businesses.

In addition, federal and state governments are initiating new policies that focus resources on workforce training and other vocational policies that align with local industries and businesses. In 2017 and 2018, for example, the presidential administration deemed apprenticeships to be a revitalized area of postsecondary training for students who do not wish to participate in traditional college programs.[16]

In addition, several states have implemented "free community college" programs, providing students who might not otherwise have access to higher education with an incentive to gain needed skills without worrying too much about the costs involved.[17]

Implications for Transfer and the Transfer Student

In this dynamic time for higher education, it would appear that the future of community colleges and the transfer function would be bright. After all, community colleges are, on average, the lowest-priced higher education segment.[18] This clearly agrees with cost-conscious families, who have made these two-year institutions among the most popular segments of US higher education.

In addition, these institutions offer a wide range of vocationally focused degrees and certificates that appeal to individuals concerned about the cost of higher education and who need a more specific trajectory from postsecondary training to a vocation following graduation. Most community colleges are keenly attuned to local labor-market trends and the workforce needs of their regions, a key competitive advantage for a public skeptical of the value of a college degree and often unwilling to shoulder its rising costs.

Although the horizon for community colleges might be bright, the future for transfer looks less positive. First, most first-time students entering a community college wish to transfer, but a large proportion never do.

The figures that are often reported to support this point are that, whereas over 80 percent of first-time college students who begin at a community college indicate a desire to transfer and earn a baccalaureate degree, less than 12 percent ever transfer to a four-year institution.[19] However, both of these figures are extremes that do not stand up to scrutiny. Yet the broad point remains: most community college students want to transfer and earn the baccalaureate, but only a small minority achieve that goal.

Transfer advocates (including the current authors) have taken comfort in these disappointing results by arguing that most community college students attend college part-time and are often not accounted for in national reports of transfer effectiveness. Up until recently, for example, the US Department of Education's IPEDS reports only reflected students who attended college on a full-time basis, which highlights that there is no uniform system for calculating transfer rates.

Other reports emphasize, quite accurately, that the time horizon used to evaluate transfer effectiveness, usually six years total, does not capture a significant number of students who earn a four-year degree within a longer time frame. The National Student Clearinghouse reports that only about 13.7 percent of community college students who transferred and earned a baccalaureate degree did so within six years.[20]

The late Cliff Adelman, in a comprehensive monograph in 2005 that tracked the enrollment trajectories of community college students thought to be focused on earning a baccalaureate degree, found that about seven in ten were successful so long as they were followed for at least twelve years.[21]

These caveats around the "true" number of successful community college transfer students are valid, and they alert the casual reader to search for the necessary nuance in reports of transfer effectiveness. Even when we dig deeper into these data, however, we cannot be pleased with the number of students who are successful in making the transition between two- and four-year institutions or the time it takes them to reach their goals.

More troubling for the future of the transfer function is the extent to which transfer is a popular and authentic educational goal of community college students. It is argued that the "popularity" of transfer—the 80 percent of incoming community college students who say they wish to transfer—is something of a mirage. Again, this figure probably represents an upper boundary, but significant survey data across several decades suggest that certainly over half and probably two-thirds of students have transfer and the baccalaureate degree as their goals.[22]

Holding aside a precise number, the underlying presumption is that community college students' intentions are not reliable—even authentic. We are told that, despite this interest in transfer, most students entering community colleges do not have the skills to earn a four-year degree. Even accounting for students whose goals may exceed their current academic grasp, it is difficult to square the enormous gap between those students who do and do not transfer as the result of individuals so unskilled that their future remains constrained to sub-baccalaureate credentials.

As for the argument that transfer students' intentions are not serious, we are told they choose the baccalaureate degree as their educational goal because that is the socially acceptable degree to which most individuals aspire.

The trouble with this explanation is that we almost never question the intentions of students who begin college at four-year institutions, even open-access institutions. If we agree that a community college represents something other than an extension of high school, then we ought to believe that students who begin there have intentions at least as serious as other students. To assume otherwise presumes a dangerous misalignment of community colleges with the overall goals of American higher education.

Another reason why transfer may be seen as less attractive to students today is community colleges' abundant offering of sub-baccalaureate credentials and degrees. Coupled with these institutions' low fees, minimal admission requirements, and geographic convenience, the presence of vocationally relevant training programs must appeal to students of all ages, but especially students from low-income backgrounds. These colleges offer a greater degree of vocational certainty—at a much lower cost—than more traditional forms of higher education.

It is then ironic that, within community colleges, there is a battle for the educational souls of their students: Who will transfer? Who will earn other kinds of sub-baccalaureate credentials?

Community college leaders will correctly say that the mission of their institutions is not singularly focused on one or the other goal. And there are data to show that the liberal arts are as robust as ever at two-year institutions.[23] But the historical division of labor at community colleges has always reinforced an uncomfortable divide that, rather than catalyze and celebrate its universalist educational mission, has instead served to create a curricular divide.

The final reason for transfer's potential decline in a post–Great Recession landscape relates to issues that have dogged the process since its earliest inception. For those of us who have been transfer advocates for decades, we must readily acknowledge that we have failed to solve the major and most obvious barrier to students' transfer capabilities: credit transfer.

Students preparing to transfer have almost no certainty that the credit they have earned at one institution will be fully accepted by the receiving institution, unless their originating and receiving institutions have developed an iron-clad articulation agreement.

In a national analysis of student transfer patterns and credit accumulation and loss, the Government Accountability Office (GAO) reported that "students lost an estimated 43 percent of college credits when they transferred," the equivalent of about 13–15 credits, or a full semester college course load.[24] The extent of lost credit varied by transfer pathway, however.

The most common path from a two-year, public institution to a four-year public lost on average about 22 percent of earned credits. This pathway—called "vertical transfer"—is the most traditional one, a trajectory that was originally sketched by the early framers of America's community colleges over a century ago. It is also routinely viewed as the place where transfer students are most likely to suffer the ill effects of credit loss, an explicit—and often deserved—criticism of four-year institutions that are seen to be disadvantaging students from community colleges.

However, the GAO report goes on to reveal that the second most popular pathway between public two-year and four-year institutions caused students to lose, on average, 69 percent of their credits. The report indicates that despite the efforts of specific states, such as Florida, to create statewide articulation agreements guaranteeing credit transfer between and among public two- and four-year institutions, a sizeable number of students in community colleges (about 30 percent) and students attending four-year institutions (25 percent) transfer out of their home state and do not benefit from these credit policies.

The point here is not to cast blame on particular segments for their credit transfer policies. There appears to be enough blame to be spread across all of higher education. The GAO report highlights that reform must include a recognition of the deeply divisive credit transfer problem that plagues transfer students, a constituency that is expected to continue to increase in the coming decades.

Of course, transfer advocates (including the current authors) can superficially comfort ourselves—in the short run—in repeating many of the reasons why credit transfer has been so difficult. Students change majors. Course content is not aligned from one institution to another. And there is insufficient guidance and insight to help students across the transfer chasm and even less communication between and among two- and four-year institutions.

Cost-conscious families care less about the reasons that transfer does not work, only that transfer—as a process—does not work. They will be uninterested in investing time and money in a process that appears disjointed, unaligned, and fragmented.

WHITHER TRANSFER?

Given the issues discussed earlier, a strong case could be made that community colleges' emphasis on transfer may be out-of-step with the post–Great Recession economic reality. Perhaps a better approach might be to divert student goals toward sub-baccalaureate degrees and certificates rather than provide access to a four-year degree.

Researchers such as James Rosenbaum at Northwestern University and his colleagues argue that a focus on transfer, especially for the majority of students who attend community colleges, is usually a failed strategy.[25] Students depart college without any credential, loading up on student debt as well. Better, he argues, to focus scarce institutional resources on academic pathways that would lead to two-year associate's degrees and workforce credentials that have labor market value. At least students would depart college with something to show for their investment of time and money.

For those who are devoted to transfer as the seminal and originating mission for community colleges, any attempt to undercut this commitment might seem immediately suspect. But Rosenbaum and others are simply making good on a contradiction we highlighted at the outset of this book. Community colleges serve the most challenged students with the fewest resources.

Almost any completion must be seen as a success, even if it is not the vaunted transfer goal that most students indicate they wish to achieve. Rosenbaum stops short of arguing that the community colleges' transfer mission should be abandoned. Nevertheless, his broader agenda is to dismantle America's focus on the "college for all" mantra, arguing that such a position inherently discourages the postsecondary intentions of students who wish to gain a toehold in the US economy without necessarily earning a four-year degree.

Holding aside the premise that a college-for-all notion is rampant in America—we would argue that the value of higher education has always been an ambivalent issue for many American families. The idea here is that higher education must simply do a better job of helping students earn postsecondary credentials and providing students who are not interested in college with other avenues for gaining a toehold in the US economy.

Simply put, abandoning transfer (or at least minimizing its importance) would divert needed resources toward a more reasonable and more focused mission for community colleges.

Given the reverberating effects of the Great Recession—the increasing cost of higher education, the uncertainty that families hold regarding the value of a college degree—should community colleges downplay or abandon access to the baccalaureate degree in service to more certain completion rates associated with less demanding and less time-consuming sub-baccalaureate degrees and certificates? Surely a case can be made for doing so. And such a move would not veer significantly from the elitist framework in which transfer was first envisioned.

However, the disadvantages of abandoning access to the baccalaureate degree are also obvious. The elimination of transfer would certainly involve community college professionals in a twenty-first-century version of "tracking," which is likely to disproportionately affect students from low-resourced backgrounds.

In the history of community colleges, there are few periods more at odds with the egalitarian spirit of the community college than the 1970s effort to encourage traditionally underrepresented students into sub-baccalaureate programs while more affluent students accessed the advantages of four-year colleges and universities via the transfer pathway.[26] During that period, transfer remained an option for all students, but the distressing outcome was that only a small proportion of students ever transferred to a four-year institution to earn a baccalaureate degree.

Even if today's rationale for focusing community college resources on more certain academic pathways is compelling, the outcome is potentially the same unless we continue to strengthen the transfer pathway and make it authentically available to students who wish to pursue a four-year degree. It is understandable that many students may not wish to earn a traditional, liberal arts degree, but we cannot consign all community colleges to this outcome, especially given their stated intentions.

WHAT IS THE VALUE OF A FOUR-YEAR DEGREE?

We have avoided until now any arguments that support the worth of a four-year degree. Of course, there is value in sub-baccalaureate credentials. Analyses by a number of organizations reveal that workers who complete two-year degrees or training certificates are likely to earn as much as $300,000 more over their lifetimes compared to individuals who gain no postsecondary training.[27]

Moreover, the current debate about the cost and value of traditional liberal art degrees has led many colleges and universities to an important and necessary reexamination of their mission and benefits. Still, the evidence is compelling that four-year degrees remain a viable—maybe the only—bulwark against economic misfortune.

Despite news reports of PhDs making lattes at Starbucks, the baccalaureate degree remains an important and pivotal entrée to the middle class.[28] It is a bet that most families continue to place as a strategy for their sons' and daughters' futures. And, indeed, those bets are properly placed. Pennsylvania State University professor David Baker could not be clearer in his assessment of rising education levels as the key driver of national and international economic and cultural advancement:

> The relationship between education and work is much studied, yet one might wonder what all the fuss is about since from everyday observations education

and work are clearly related. Indeed, that is what a virtual mountain of systemic research shows in nation after nation, then as well as now, and without exception across the whole literature: all else equal, on average, workers with more education earn more income than less educated workers.[29]

The future of work is "upskilling" and lifelong learning. The pace of change is too quick, and the needs of the economy too diverse. Joseph E. Aoun, in his book *Robot-Proof: Higher Education in the Age of Artificial Intelligence*, notes that "one estimate from the World Economic Forum claims that 65 percent of children entering primary school today will eventually work in jobs that do not [yet] exist."[30]

But beyond the ever-present economic motive that seems to dominate the discussion around the value of postsecondary education, Aoun emphasizes that "[t]o stay relevant in an AI [artificial intelligence] economy, lifelong learning will be an imperative for all professionals—and not only professionals. By helping everyone develop and maintain valuable skills, lifelong learning is necessary to alleviate social inequality."[31]

By definition, upskilling and lifelong learning will demand that individuals attend multiple institutions over the course of their lifetime. Few families in America today stay in one place for long. As a result, traditional higher education trajectories will be disrupted and new ones will be created. There are those who see student "swirling" as problematic for students who wish to earn a terminal degree, but the future looks like it will place a premium on this strategy.

We have learned in other parts of this book about the changing landscape of higher education. In chapter 7, there was an extensive discussion about online learning. We addressed in chapter 4 the growing demand for different kinds of college credit, from AP to DE. In chapters 5 and 6, we discussed the trend toward competency-based education and the need to acknowledge prior-learning experience in some fashion. With these changes come new avenues of transfer.

The traditional two- to four-year school trajectory will not go away but will be accompanied by other pathways. If we are going to see those new pathways thrive, we will need to ensure that the problems students face now with transfer be solved.

Still, for us, there is a more compelling issue at the heart of the dilemma we face, and it is not in assessing the labor-market value of a degree. Rather, it is in claiming the humanistic imperative of postsecondary education itself. Without resorting to the histrionics that this debate seems to arouse, is it unreasonable to remind ourselves that college was designed to be something more than an employment office for industry?

Today, the considerable time and attention devoted to discussing the inherent "worthiness" of committing our sons and daughters to time in college classrooms illustrates an inchoate and uneasy, even existential, distress at the center of the national psyche about investing in our national culture that claims no annual dividend.

Ironically, Anthony Carnevale, one of the US leaders advancing the debate that places postsecondary education squarely on the shoulders of a utilitarian calculus of labor market needs and personal economic necessities, holds the broader debate aloft as well as anyone:

> Putting meat on the bones of the populist notion of "college for all" is the new frontier in meeting the equally cherished goals of merit and opportunity. If we can't operationalize the notion of "college for all" in a way that balances our commitment to merit and opportunity, education runs the risk of becoming a passive participant in a system that fosters the intergenerational reproduction of economic and cultural elites.[32]

Acknowledging an uncertain national commitment to the fundamental goals of higher education that include at least something in addition to the world of work, University of Illinois professor of economics Walter W. McMahon draws a reasoned and ecumenical conclusion after an extensive analysis of the public and private benefits of higher education:

> The goal of a new higher education policy needs to contribute efficiently to graduates' and society's longer-term private and social benefits in ways that include but are not limited to earnings. It also needs to relate these benefits to the costs of higher education to continually evaluate cost-effectiveness, efficiency, and accountability. When this is done, the conclusion is that higher education investment, public and private, is below its optimum. Sustained underinvestment has its price. Human capital formation through education, including higher education, over time does determine the future. And yet higher education and with it the greater good are at risk. This puts the nation at risk.[33]

That investment and that risk are described in the next two chapters.

Chapter 9

Tomorrowland

Proven Pathways Forward

"It's ethically irresponsible not to start with a certificate-first program."

—Clark Gilbert, president of
BYU Pathway Worldwide[1]

The educational landscape has become increasingly complex in twenty-first-century America, as the preceding chapters have illustrated. Academic credit frequently begins to be accumulated by students in high school, whether in the form of IB, AP, early college high school (ECHS), or other dual credit.

The mélange of college credit earned while in high school would, no doubt, be a shock to community college "founder" William Rainey Harper and his firmly held belief that community college should be an extension of high school, rather than the other way around. It never occurred to Harper that students would be allowed (let alone encouraged) to accumulate college credit in high school.

Academic credit earned in high school, of course, has been further expanded. It began with ACE, which created a process for the awarding of academic credit for knowledge accumulated during World War II military service.

More recently, the implementation and successful usage of PLA have become increasingly accepted across the United States, whether for work-based learning or other learning outside of the classroom. CBE is another nascent educational model being developed in numerous variations. Of course, all of these forms of credit are transferred and stacked toward degrees, and this complicated, swirling credit-accumulation landscape has been further impacted by the current unprecedented growth in online education.

Given the variety of educational models and the wide range of possibilities that they hold in the twenty-first century, where should the United States invest its educational dollars? Should we continue, via submerged tax code benefits to corporate entities and with our federal financial aid policies, to fund corporate/institutional partnerships of the ASU/Starbucks variety (see chapter 7), or might more promising and equitable alternatives be replicated from other successful, existing models?

Although there are compelling, evidence-based models that call for national expansion and replication as highly effective educational pathways, they are not as well known by the American public as they should be. These laudatory programs share a common design element. They seek to stack previously earned transfer credits alongside newly earned credits into life-changing credentials and degrees. Importantly, these programs all recognize the predominance of neo-traditional students—and all of the numerous life challenges they navigate—as their primary audience.

Intentional design components recognize and mitigate these life challenges as part of these holistic educational models. Brigham Young University's PathwayConnect, Rhode Island's College Unbound, City University of New York's Accelerated Study in Associates Program, and Los Angeles Valley College's Family Resource Center provide four exemplary model frameworks that foster student success and serve the country as anti-poverty strategies at scale.

Notably, rather than lining the pockets of for-profit education investors, as certainly signaled by ASU's newly created for-profit "corporate partnership arm,"[2] these models strive both to keep costs low for students and to provide high-quality, comprehensive student- and family-centered support that extends from recruitment through graduation. The focus is not merely on access to college but also on a lower cost-per-degree earned. Arguably, this is the metric that matters most to individuals, to their families, and to a society focused on its return for investment in education.

PATHWAYCONNECT AND A MOTTO
OF "NO CREDIT LEFT BEHIND"

PathwayConnect is a year-long, fifteen-credit "educational on-ramp" program created by Brigham Young University. PathwayConnect was expressly crafted to encourage both traditional and neo-traditional students to enter (or re-enter) college.

From the student perspective, PathwayConnect embodies a compelling "no credit left behind" message and approach, designed to ensure that every credential will stack into a full bachelor's degree without any loss of credit.

For example, a modest certificate in sales produces 14 credit hours that may be applied toward the 60-credit associate's degree, which then feeds directly into the 120-credit bachelor's degree in business management.[3] Over 40,000 students have already graduated from the program, with half of those graduates funneled directly into a BYU-Idaho online certificate or degree.[4]

Although PathwayConnect is oriented toward serving students of the Mormon faith in its current iteration, the most salient components are highly replicable regardless of institutional type. Deeply attractive to students is the price of only $73 per credit hour (with a price point that is even lower if the student is overseas). This low cost continues onto the baccalaureate if the student continues her or his education via BYU-Online, which has doubtless fueled BYU-Online's dramatic growth over the past five years.

The affordability of a PathwayConnect degree is a substantial bargain: the total cost is $8,100 for the 120 credits required for a bachelor's degree, and this is especially impressive in an era when the "$10,000 degree" continues be considered the elusive ideal.[5] The degree is inexpensive for two reasons.

First, rather than relying on expensive search-engine optimization, arranging for steeply priced ad words, and purchasing pricey digital marketing, PathwayConnect maintains spectacularly low recruitment costs for student acquisition, because most students hear about the program by word-of-mouth from the church. Second, this affordable price point is possible because of a heavy reliance on adjunct instructors supplemented by church volunteers.

PathwayConnect utilizes a highly effective, mixed modality pedagogical approach. (See also the discussion of online education in chapter 7.) Its online instruction is supplemented by mandatory weekly meetings, which are subdivided into sections for those below and those above the age of thirty years, in recognition of the shifting challenges of pursuing higher education at different stages of life.

In this hybrid pedagogical approach, each student takes a turn "leading" the group in a review of the work covered the previous week. These weekly gatherings are supplemented by advising and tutoring offered by church volunteers. This aspect of community-building is a strong positive, and it can prove to be a central animating life-force for students who need support and affirmation for their efforts. In a less sectarian environment, the implementation of this component may resemble the "peer-led team learning" (PLTL) model.[6]

The PathwayConnect program combines online courses with weekly local church or institute gatherings. A program of the Church of Jesus Christ of Latter-day Saints, "PathwayConnect is a reduced-cost online program that prepares students to start or finish a degree by building spiritual confidence and teaching foundational academic skills."[7]

Some potential students are doubtless put off by the prospect of a "gospel-incorporated education" (as well as the two-course sequence covering the Book of Mormon), and in response the church has created new PathwayConnect programs for non-church members with a connection to the church at thirty-five sites.[8] Regardless of religious affiliation, the most powerful and replicable component of PathwayConnect is certainly its "certificate first," no-credit-left-behind ideology and curricular strategy.

Powerfully, the student is working "toward" a credential from the very start, and the stackable nature of the curriculum means that the student may also benefit from multiple entry and exit points. With this intentional curricular redesign, general education courses are not offered until after the student earns an initial certificate. This is the opposite of a typical degree program, which tends to feature general education courses for the first year or two of collegiate study.

This flipped curricular approach has led to dramatic improvements for at-risk students. Students who earn a certificate first are retained at the rate of 85 percent, significantly higher than the 65 percent who have not earned a certificate.[9] Clark Gilbert, the president of BYU Pathway Worldwide, believes that this powerful curricular redesign is the best way to serve Pathway students, 70 percent of whom are first-generation college students, low-income students, or both.[10]

Gilbert has gone so far as to state that "it's ethically irresponsible not to start with a certificate-first program."[11] Retention and graduation data clearly indicate that PathwayConnect's flipped-model curricular innovation results in powerful retention gains for the most at-risk students.

Certainly, as we address persistent, intergenerational inequalities in higher education, this is a template for consideration, adaption, and replication that recognizes the reality that not every student will ultimately want to complete a bachelor's degree. However, the credits they earn along the way should always stack into a credential that will improve their job prospects and earning potential. This approach also facilitates a return to college when (and if) the student wishes to pursue the next academic credential.

THE SOCIAL JUSTICE ANCHORING
OF COLLEGE UNBOUND

Rhode Island's private, nonprofit College Unbound institution was founded in 2009 with a mission that has evolved to focus on degree completion for neo-traditional students. Specifically focused on transfer students, College Unbound highlights an admissions requirement that an applicant must have previously earned a minimum of nine college credits.

College Unbound was created by Dennis Littky, an education innovator who was frustrated that many neo-traditional students were not succeeding at traditional universities and colleges.[12] Currently, no tuition is charged to the student for the College Unbound Solo program; funding from the Lumina Foundation and other donors covers the cost-per-degree of $10,000. The goal is to have every student graduate debt-free with grants, scholarships, and donations.[13]

At present, 90 percent of the institution's budget is funded from donations, foundations, and grants rather than tuition.[14] This percentage will doubtless change because the college recently became eligible for accreditation by the New England Commission of Higher Education, making students eligible for federal financial aid. (Over 80 percent of College Unbound students are Pell Grant–eligible, so this will be significant moving forward.)

Most impressively, unlike the many for-profit institutions discussed in chapter 7, the graduation rate for College Unbound currently stands at a stunning 80 percent. This model is distinct in several ways. College Unbound offers a single, highly flexible bachelor's degree in organizational leadership that is project-driven around an individual student's interests.

The degree program utilizes both PLA and CBE. Students enroll in cohorts of ten to fifteen, in semesters that are divided into two focused eight-week terms of six courses.[15] Cohorts are formed, and groups of students meet every week (with no summer break) across the state of Rhode Island, in locations that bring education directly to students, including ten employer on-site programs such as the United Way in Providence, where employees gather in their office building after work for class.[16]

Additional student supports are offered that mirror those of a traditional college, including psychologists, learning specialists, writing and math tutors, and mental health providers. College Unbound also recognizes that the vast majority of its students are working adults with families, and the institutional response to this is both practical as well as principled.

Class attendance is intentionally supported by providing both free food and free childcare for every weekly class meeting. Given the recent findings of Temple University's national survey that 45 percent of college students (and over half of community college students) experienced food insecurity within the preceding thirty days, providing food along with childcare is a remarkable level of support.[17]

The conceptual design of the institution is also striking. Rather than re-working existing structures, the creation of a new college with a neo-traditional student-centric approach facilitated the creation of a one-stop approach toward all student services. A single cross-trained advisor is able to help a student register and pay for classes, apply for financial aid, and receive both advising and career planning and placement.

The design element of a single cross-trained advisor is certainly replicable; this approach ensures that a student is not discouraged as he or she navigates from office to office. This student-centric model is an important element, one that many for-profit institutions have leveraged to great effect. However, unlike for-profit institutions, College Unbound provides a shared sense of community and actively encourages the success of students with such support as the free childcare and free food mentioned above.

In addition to a personal advisor, free childcare, and free meals, many of the high-impact practices that we know work—from the creation of learning communities to the utilization of capstone projects and the awarding of credit for prior learning—are fundamental design components of College Unbound, rather than institutional additions or adjustments to existing structures.

College Unbound is student-centered to a level that is, frankly, stunning. The current graduation rate of 80 percent is truly groundbreaking, especially when we consider the students (and their families) whose lives are transformed.

And who is the typical College Unbound student? The demographics of College Unbound students reflect the national neo-traditional student profile. The average age is thirty-eight years; 69 percent are female; 79 percent are students of color; 80 percent work full-time; and 74 percent are Pell Grant–eligible.[18] College Unbound's mission is to "reinvent higher education for underrepresented returning adult learners, using a model that is individualized, interest-based, project-driven, workplace-enhanced, cohort-supported, flexible, supportive, and affordable."[19] This is a remarkable attempt to fulfill that lofty aspiration.

President Littky sees enrollment rapidly increasing, and he has hopes of expanding into a national and perhaps international market.[20] College Unbound utilizes both PLA and CBE; provides additional insights and replicable models for effective, holistic educational structures, including a single-advisor student services structure; and offers a compressed curricular model that is driven by student interest and experience.

THE ACCELERATED STUDY IN ASSOCIATES PROGRAMS MODEL

Another impressive, successful set of interventions is demonstrated by the City University of New York's (CUNY) Accelerated Study in Associates Programs (ASAP) model. This research-validated model combines face-to-face instruction with a holistic array of "wrap around" student services. ASAP was formed in 2007 as a groundbreaking partnership between CUNY and New York City's Office of the Mayor.

The primary aim of ASAP centers on "the explicit goal of addressing poverty by improving educational outcomes for low-income students."[21] Indeed, the vast majority of ASAP students are low-income, with more than 80 percent of the participants receiving Pell Grants.[22] ASAP is designed to be a comprehensive program that addresses multiple barriers to student success. It is aimed at increasing associate's degree attainment, fostering successful transfer into four-year degree programs, and dramatically improving subsequent career earnings.

In order to participate, students must agree to a specific list of requirements. Full-time enrollment is required, as is a commitment to participating in a wide range of financial, academic, and personal supports. Programming includes personalized advisement (by advisors with reduced caseloads), tutoring, counseling, tuition waivers, and waivers of mandatory fees.

Free transportation is provided via the distribution of pre-paid Metropolitan Transportation Authority/New York City Transit MetroCards; students must meet with their advisor in order to access their MetroCard. Additional financial assistance is provided to defray the cost of textbooks.

The ASAP model supplements this broad array of student services with intentional and broad structural shifts in academic affairs. Institutional redesign of ASAP features prioritized class scheduling options, cohort-building classes with other ASAP students, and "block scheduling" of classes designed to accommodate student work schedules. Students receive additional supports as they near graduation to help them either transfer to four-year colleges or transition into the workforce.

A rigorous external evaluation of the ASAP model included an analysis of the most recent five cohorts with graduation data for fall 2009, spring 2010, fall 2010, fall 2011, and fall 2012. Using propensity score matching, this analysis found that ASAP students had a three-year graduation rate of 52.4 percent, which was much higher than the comparison group graduation rate of 26.8 percent. In addition, ASAP students had a higher two-year graduation rate (24.4 percent versus 8.4 percent), and those students who graduated within three years completed their degrees in slightly less time (4.7 semesters compared to 5.0 semesters on average).[23]

Furthermore, according to internal research, ASAP effects held regardless of race/ethnicity or gender and for Pell Grant recipients. This internal analysis revealed that "African American male students in ASAP had a three-year graduation rate of 47.0 percent (versus 20.8 percent for the comparison group), Hispanic male students had a rate of 46.7 percent (versus 18.2 percent), and Pell recipients a rate of 52.7 percent (versus 27.3 percent)."[24]

This internal study was further validated by external research conducted by MDRC, a nonprofit, nonpartisan organization. Its examination utilized an experimental (random assignment) design, with the aim of reducing selection bias. The study found "nearly double the three-year graduation rate of control group students, at 40.1 percent versus 21.8 percent, an effect of 18.3 percentage points."[25] The authors note that "ASAP's effects are the largest MDRC has found in more than a decade of research in higher education."[26]

This stunning report confirms that ASAP students outperform the control group on every metric imaginable: higher rates of enrollment, higher levels of credits earned, and higher rates of transfer to four-year institutions. Of course, the high levels of student support that are imperative to ASAP prove expensive at the outset. However, the returns are persuasively high, and the cost-per-degree is actually significantly lower.

Several studies confirm the cost-benefits of the ASAP model. Essentially, even allowing for the higher cost of instruction and support, there is a lower cost-per-degree awarded because of the dramatic increase in graduation rates of ASAP students. One study conducted at the Center for Benefit-Cost Studies in Education at Teachers College, Columbia University, by Henry M. Levin and Emma García, found that the cost per graduate for ASAP students resulted in savings of "$6,500 per graduate for the ASAP cohort relative to the comparison group."[27]

A second benefit-analysis by the same authors found impressive wide-ranging additional benefits, including substantially increased lifetime earnings and tax revenues, and corresponding decreases in spending on public assistance, public health, and the criminal justice system that translated into a whopping return of $3 to $4 for every $1 invested in ASAP.[28] In addition, the study cited earlier by Strumbos, Linderman, and Hicks notes:

> For first-time freshmen, the ASAP student transfer rate was 19 percent higher than the comparison group and the bachelor's degree attainment rate was 49 percent higher. This suggests that ASAP not only helps students earn their associate degrees, but also helps them transfer and better prepares them for success in earning the bachelor's degree, even more critical for long-term economic mobility.[29]

Clearly, the ASAP model requires a substantial initial investment but results in remarkable gains in degree production.

Inspired by ASAP and the research confirming its efficacy, others have moved forward with replication of its model. Of special note is the collaboration among three community colleges in Ohio that have implemented ASAP's prototype. MDRC was engaged from the beginning in exploring whether or not the ASAP model was truly replicable.

Key components of the ASAP design were maintained. Students were required to enroll full-time, encouraged to complete any developmental courses, and provided with a broad array of support services, most importantly intensive mandatory advising. Blocked courses and compressed schedules were also maintained.

Financial supports, including free textbooks and, instead of MetroCards, a $50 gas/grocery card to incentivize advisor meetings, were also key common design principles. Interested and eligible students were selected by random assignment either into the program or into the control group.

And the results? According to a policy brief by MDRC, "Graduation rates more than doubled: 19 percent of the program group earned a degree or credential after two years compared with 8 percent of the control group."[30] This improvement is remarkable, especially given the student body demographics.

About half of the students were neo-traditional. About three-fourths of the students required developmental education courses. And almost two-thirds of the students were employed during the time of their enrollment. All of the participating students were Pell Grant–eligible. As the policy brief authors remark:

> [T]he Ohio demonstration provides evidence that the model can work in a different context and with a different student population, as many more students in Ohio were nontraditional. These findings further validate the effectiveness of the CUNY ASAP model and add to the growing body of evidence on effective strategies for improving the educational outcomes of low-income students.[31]

Other colleges in both New York and California have begun to roll out ASAP-like programs, with technical assistance from CUNY. The expansion of the model will add to the growing body of evidence for the effectiveness of a holistic, student-centric approach. The results are inspirational, with the doubling of graduation rates for students with the lowest socioeconomic status. However, the fact remains that, whether in New York or Ohio, successful program graduates constitute only half of the students that desire a degree or certificate. The majority fail to achieve their academic dream.

There is much more work to be done to ensure that the bulk of students who want a degree are sufficiently supported to attain their goal. Any conversation around "free college" (in the wide variety of implementation models currently under discussion) should not be decoupled from a conversation about the design models that have actually been proven to work and about the percentage of students who complete a degree.

How should the United States best support higher education in a manner that results in a lower cost-per-degree? Additional programming, both at CUNY and at Los Angeles Valley College, provide powerful hints about how best to support degree competition.

CUNY's Single Stop College Initiative is a remarkable integrative effort that supplements ASAP. The initiative utilizes a fifteen-minute intake survey that ascertains which federal, state, and local benefits students are eligible to receive, including health insurance programs, nutrition programs, housing assistance, childcare subsidies, tax credits, and energy assistance.[32] On-site Single Stop counselors then assist the student through the various benefit application processes.

Single Stop additionally provides tax preparation, financial counseling, and legal counseling. Sixty-one percent of students served are female, 45 percent work at least full-time, and 38 percent are parents. In short, Single Stop's comprehensive services are bringing holistic support similar to those being offered in K–12 by numerous nonprofit organizations, including the thirty-year-old Say Yes to Education. This level of programming is implemented with the full realization that, for many students, academic challenges are only one of the many obstacles they face.

THE "PARENT STUDENT" APPROACH AT
LOS ANGELES VALLEY COLLEGE

In addition to the food insecurity issue mentioned previously, a growing percentage of neo-traditional students are parents, balancing the care of their children alongside the pursuit of their education. As noted in a 2016 Institute for Women's Policy Research brief, 4.8 million Americans are now undergraduate parent-students.[33] And these numbers are on the rise. From 1995 to 2012, the number of parent-students grew dramatically from 3.2 million to 4.8 million, with 89 percent of parent-student families defined as low income.[34]

Parent-students are found, as we might expect, in US community colleges; however, the increase in parent-students has been occurring across all institutional types and in all regions of the country.[35] It may be hard to believe, but 26 percent of the US undergraduate student population is simultaneously raising children—over one-quarter of the nation's undergraduates.[36]

These parent-students are most likely to be female (71 percent).[37] In the community college, these percentages are, not surprisingly, even higher, where nearly one in three community college students is also a parent.[38] Traditionally underrepresented community members are also more likely to be parent-students. Nearly half of all Black women, one-third of Hispanic women, and two-fifths of Native American and Native-Hawaiian/Pacific-Islander women are student-mothers.[39]

Many parent-students face the substantial additional challenge of single parenthood: 43 percent of US parent-students are single mothers, and 11 percent are single fathers.[40] That over 50 percent of parent-students are also single parents is important to underscore, because the impact of single parenthood on degree completion is dramatic. Only 8 percent of single mothers complete an associate's or bachelor's degree within six years.[41] As a point of comparison, roughly 50 percent of undergraduate students without children are likely to graduate within the same timeframe.[42]

Addressing the needs of parent-students is absolutely vital if we are to positively "move the dial" on both racial/ethnic and income inequality. With the dramatic impact of parenting, especially single parenting, on student success, and with the growing numbers of neo-traditional students, different types of investments (rather than a generic "free college" approach) will be required in order to provide access along with the critical support that leads to the successful completion of a college credential.

One model, found at Los Angeles Valley College, provides a replicable and successful template. In a recent interview, the director of the Family Resource Center at Los Angeles Valley College, Marni Roosevelt, summarizes the mindset shift that is required to more comprehensively and effectively foster student success:

> We know that student-parents are really parents first. They're really parent-students. And that the second that something happens within their family, that means they have to stop going to school. They have to choose between family or school, they're gonna choose family. So we know that the only way to support the student is also to support their kids.[43]

Similar to the College Unbound model described earlier, the Family Resource Center offers "an academic counselor, after school (school-age) childcare, a lactation room with a refrigerator for breast milk, a kid-friendly study lounge, tutoring, textbook support, computer and printing access, school supplies, a children's clothing exchange, organic produce, diapers/wipes/formula, and so much more."[44]

This comprehensive parent-student approach means that the center staff also includes a marriage/family therapist and a social worker. And it is successful: 80 percent of the Los Angeles Valley College students engaged with the center complete their semester, compared to a completion rate of 69 percent across campus.[45]

Although these efforts are currently funded primarily through philanthropy and not yet scaled, both the public good and private good returns are significant. As researcher Lindsey Reichlin Cruse of the Institute for Women's Policy Research confirmed:

> The investment that single mothers make in their college education more than pays off in the returns—once they graduate. So for associate's degrees, it's about $16.50 to one. For every dollar a single mother invests in college, she gets $16.50 back

over her lifetime. And over that lifetime, that adds up to around $330,000 more than she would have made with only a high school diploma. There are significant tax contributions, to the tune of nearly $8 billion, over the lifetime of all the single mothers expected to graduate with a degree. And public assistance savings would be in excess of $310 million, just in the four years after they graduate.[46]

These fiscal benefits are compelling. Together with SUNY's ASAP and the College Unbound models, the Family Resource Center model underscores that, though the initial costs are indeed higher, broad family-focused strategic and intentional investments provide a significant return in the long run.

Rather than the blunt instrument of the "free college" movement, these models collectively underscore that we as a nation need to provide significantly more. Without the addition of a wide array of intentional and comprehensive supports designed especially for students and for their families, these educational investments will continue to fall far short of their potential. Worse, given that currently only 8 percent of single parent-students complete their degree, we miss the opportunity to provide the intergenerational benefits that result from successful degree completion.

In addition to the higher earnings and the benefits of those resources, research has found that educational achievement by single parents results in additional benefits, including greater involvement in their children's education and the increased chances of their child pursuing college, too.[47]

However, the Family Resource Center is not (yet) standard. Currently, it is the only such center at a community college in the entire state of California.[48] To truly be equity-driven, state or federal "free college" programs must first invest in low-income students and, utilizing the comprehensive parent-student approach epitomized in the Family Resource Center, fund a vast array of non-tuition expenses for low-income students.

Our nation's neo-traditional students want—and deserve—to access the transformative promise of higher education. Our national conception of college affordability simply must extend beyond a singular focus on cost.

We must consider all of the facets that affect low-income students' ability not only to enter college but also to persist and graduate, from help in navigating food and housing insecurity to addressing the myriad demands of being a parent-student. The promise of our democracy depends on it. The four models outlined earlier present enticing possibilities for forging solutions at scale.

SERVING NEO-TRADITIONAL
STUDENTS: COMMON ELEMENTS

In these four models—BYU's PathwayConnect, Rhode Island's College Unbound, CUNY's ASAP combined with the Single Stop College Initiative, and Los Angeles Valley College's Family Resource Center—several common elements foster success for the nation's neo-traditional students.

Not incidentally, and perhaps not surprisingly, all of these approaches are based in community colleges and place a strong emphasis on the facilitated transfer of academic credit. This reality demands that the United States should dedicate even more attention to ensuring a robust and flexible approach to the transfer function, both at the two-year college and at the four-year receiving institution. We must establish guided pathways throughout the entire undergraduate educational experience in ways that truly mean no loss of time, money, or academic credit for all students.

Almost all of these approaches include redesigned curricula, resulting in condensed scheduling blocks designed to accommodate the schedules of working students, or a completely reworked curricula utilizing BYU's approach where "every credit counts." This flipped curriculum design begins with market-focused credentials that immediately enhance earning potential while providing a stackable credential designed to fold directly into an associate's or bachelor's degree.

The realization that every student may not want to continue into a bachelor's degree is celebrated, as is the realization that even some college, as long as it results in a credential, greatly enhances employability and earnings. This redesign mitigates the potentially deleterious impacts of leaving college without earning a degree, since valuable credentials are earned "along the way."

The embrace of PLA and CBE in the College Unbound model further underscores the importance of recognizing all academic credit earned, both for the traditional undergraduate desiring academic credit for his or her internship and for academic credit earned in the military or in the workforce by the neo-traditional student.

All of these approaches offer intensive academic supports in addition to a vast array of life supports that range from lactation support, child care, and counseling to assistance with navigating food and housing insecurity. Almost all of these approaches celebrate the formation of learning communities, which are designed to motivate and celebrate transformed lives (and the lives of their families) through education.

These comprehensive elements may look radically different from what we are "used to seeing" for students attending a traditional four-year institution. The rapidly shifting needs of US students require permanent, ongoing funding that supports academic access and just-in-time student services along a holistic, whole-life continuum.

Although the initial outlay may seem substantial, maintaining a clear focus on a lower cost-per-degree will provide the financial justification for these investments. Even more powerfully, the undeniable educational, societal, and financial rewards for all students is a meritorious promise that upholds and embodies the highest and best ideals of American democracy.

Chapter 10

Beyond Traditional Transfer

Findings and Recommendations

"While there are, and will continue to be, intensive public debates about all aspects of education and from many different political ideologies, these rarely if ever conclude that less education for individuals and the collective is the best path."

—David P. Baker, *The Schooled Society*[1]

There is something very positive stirring in American higher education. Hard questions are being posed by policymakers, journalists, and families alike: What is the value of a college degree? How much should it cost? What is the proper investment of the state and federal government in this enterprise? How long should it take to earn a credential or degree? We are engaged in a lively debate, grappling with issues that touch the core of our work.

If we are true to ourselves and the mission of our institutions, we must accept that some elements need improvement, that our current methods may need modification, and that our engagement with policymakers and neo-traditional families, far from holding a defensive or apologetic posture, must double-down on the transformative aspect of postsecondary education.

THEN AGAIN: BEYOND TRADITIONAL TRANSFER

We began with a simple thesis for this book: How can we improve the hundred-year-old transfer pathway between community colleges and four-year institutions? But our thinking and our writing took us elsewhere, to a broader set of issues, revealing an unsettling constellation of findings and necessitating a more ambitious set of recommendations.

119

It is our belief that the higher education trends we describe here will not simply alter the transfer landscape but will—in fact, are—reshaping higher education generally. Of course, we are not the first to document these changes, and we have highlighted the work of talented researchers and thinkers throughout this book.

In this concluding chapter, we share a summary of our findings and a series of recommendations. Our transfer-advocate colleagues may be puzzled by the generality of our claims and strategies but will, we think, immediately appreciate their relevance. More than most, they will understand that without consideration of these recommendations in some fashion, all students will continue to be saddled with a system that serves institutions more effectively than the students who attend them—and, candidly, serves neither especially well.

As participants in higher education most of our adult lives, we understand the survival instinct of colleges and universities. Our recommendations do not insist that institutions hobble themselves in a standards-less accommodation of student needs at any cost. We do believe, however, that there are important institution-specific changes that can be implemented to allow students attending multiple institutions to plug into degrees and certifications that will advance them economically and culturally while sustaining or enhancing the quality of the US higher education enterprise.

Beyond local institutional change, there is growing interest by state and federal leaders in developing policy strategies that increase student access to college and, presumably, increase completion rates. We could not be more pleased that education is back on the front burner of political debate, even if that debate is sometimes shrill and simplistic.

Our starting point is the discussion occurring around "free college." The possibility of attending college for little or no cost has instant and broad appeal, and it has many supporters. Various states currently offer versions of "free college," and although these programs do increase degree production, they are not nearly as effective as programs supplemented with more substantial academic and life supports (as discussed in chapter 9).

At the heart of these efforts is an energy and desire to re-invest in the transformative promise of higher education. We applaud this renewed commitment to postsecondary education, but insist that such initiatives be combined with investments that result in greater numbers of students completing degrees and certificates. That we may disagree with the specifics of generic "free college" initiatives will soon be evident, but this should not be viewed as anything other than an argument among allies.

Investing in the Baccalaureate

A good deal of the rhetoric around free college is focused on helping students earn sub-baccalaureate degrees and credentials. Much less has been said about elevating the educational prospects of students who wish to transfer and earn a four-year degree.

We understand that emphasis—indeed, support it—so long as the transfer mission remains an indelible part of the community college mission. Authentic access to the baccalaureate degree is the goal of most new students attending community colleges, and, though many may find other satisfying educational trajectories, this pathway must remain available and viable.

In our view, transfer (and student attainment of the baccalaureate degree) remains the most transformative aspect of the community college mission. It is not, however, the most efficient pathway toward that goal, as we described in chapter 8. First-time college students are far more likely to earn a baccalaureate degree if they begin college at a four-year institution, and not at a community college.

If policymakers and community college leaders believe that transfer is a sidelight amid other two-year college missions—given the recent emphasis on workforce degrees and certificates—then we should highlight the challenge now. Every transfer challenge we have discussed in this book—credit transfer probably the most central—disappears if we choose to abandon the transfer function.

This radical approach, however, is likely to disenfranchise neo-traditional students from attending higher education at all. They may well earn a certificate or a two-year degree but will be effectively closed off from advancing further academically. Without investment in a comprehensive transfer pathway, many students will be denied access to a four-year degree, the ticket universally understood as required to gain entrée to a wider world of economic and cultural possibility.

What are those investments? Throughout this book, we have highlighted strategies that will enhance educational equality by fostering the replication of research-tested models that systemically support student success and graduation, especially for the students most at risk of not achieving their educational dream. A student from the bottom quartile of income has only an 11 percent likelihood of completing college.[2] Put another way, without strategic and dramatic investment, nearly 90 percent of students from the lowest income quartile will fail to graduate.

As the United States becomes more sensitive to the costs associated with low graduation rates, legislators have responded by instituting various performance-based funding models. These models are designed to reward practices that boost certificate and degree productivity. But the extra funds garnered are not sufficient to significantly improve the completion rates of our most challenged students. Moreover, institutions may circumvent such policies by admitting better prepared students, tactics that contradict the egalitarian aims of open-access postsecondary institutions.

As a nation, we must guarantee that access to higher education also includes the necessary academic and life supports, comprehensive services that despite their higher initial costs actually reduce the cost-per-degree by increasing degree production. The US student body is rapidly changing, and our embrace of these new populations must mirror these changes.

The convergence, then, of our thinking is a dramatic but historically resonant ideal. In 1945, this nation faced a similar educational imperative, an urgency to meet the specific needs of American citizens in a manner that was visionary, comprehensive, and research driven. Returning US veterans needed to be educated for a post-war economy, lest the nation be saddled with millions of individuals unskilled for life and unable to support their families.

Thus, the G.I. Bill was created as an intentional, strategic, and wholly social construction to solidify the nation's middle class. As Cornell University political scientist Suzanne Mettler notes:

> The tragedy is that this policy, which expanded social opportunity so powerfully a half-century ago, lacks a successor with comparable impact today. The losses accrue not only in terms of forfeited educational advancement and enhanced socioeconomic status for many lower- and middle-class Americans but also in terms of their civic engagement and political participation, the very life-blood of American democracy itself.[3]

Today, the vast majority of students are not returning from war. But the economic challenges they face—domestically and internationally—are similar to those veterans and are as significant to the economic and cultural health of our nation.

Like those veterans, most students are certainly not rich, possess few disposable assets, and often need to support a family. And like those veterans, many of them will earn a degree using whatever variant of "night school" applies in the twenty-first century. Should we not invest in these students as we did for our World War II veterans? US colleges and universities met that challenge half a century ago. It is no exaggeration to believe that the long-term economic conditions today are just as dire, and the future of the middle class is no less threatened.

FINDINGS AND RECOMMENDATIONS

Throughout the findings and recommendations to follow, we emphasize two overarching worldviews:

- That specific, strategic investments must be judged by cost-per-degree as the controlling metric; and
- That degree completion should always be our aim even as we celebrate the necessity of open-access institutions.

These guiding views will require radical shifts in our educational models, especially if we are interested in advancing a just and ethical higher educational compact to the public. The goal is not to get students through the door of postsecondary education; after all, open-access institutions successfully recruit new students every day. Rather, the goal is to ensure that students leave with the degree or credential they arrived seeking, and in a fashion that honors the investment of US taxpayers.

The outcomes and recommendations to follow are informed by the research of the many talented scholars and higher education leaders we have cited throughout this book. We encourage you to delve more deeply into the preceding chapters for more details and full source references, but we also hope that the distilled descriptions given here prove helpful.

Finding 1: The Goal Is Completion, not Access-as-Birthright

Although attractive, access to higher education without the necessary supports to help students succeed will not address the fundamental inequalities of our higher educational system. It is also unfair to taxpayers who, generous in their view of the transformative qualities of higher education, have come to expect more from students and colleges and universities. Current "free college" proposals appear to expand access without helping students advance themselves toward the completion of degrees and credentials.

Access to higher education is not enough, because the completion of a credential and subsequent graduation is necessary in order to harness the benefits of a college education. Unfortunately, many of our nation's most underprepared students enter college but fail to achieve their desired degree.

Tragically, these low graduation rates mean that many students depart without an earnings-enhancing credential in hand and yet are burdened with substantial student loan debt. This is a toxic recipe for higher education and the nation, and it has contributed to the dashing of the dreams of individuals as well as wavering support by the public. We believe that US educational investments must be more strategic and more comprehensive.

Recommendation A: Incentivize students to complete rigorous, honors-level courses in high school.

In chapter 3, we described the pernicious effects of low expectations, especially for students who see no link between working hard in high school and entering college. Their perception is correct. Even mediocre performance in high school is no barrier to enrollment in open-access institutions. Research shows, however, that preparing students with a rigorous high school curriculum provides substantial boosts to college success, both in terms of reducing collegiate time-to-degree and increasing completion rates. However, these positive impacts are only present if certain conditions are met.

AP and IB programming has been shown to be highly effective. Both AP and IB implementation requires rigorous teacher training and national standards that encourage the offering of the demanding high school curriculum that has been repeatedly proven to ensure future academic success.

Recommendation B: Ensure that these honors-level courses are available to all students regardless of high school location.

We must challenge ourselves as a country to provide rigorous educational opportunities in every K–12 school, not just the schools fortunate enough to be located in well-resourced areas. With strong positive outcomes already established but currently only selectively implemented, we must insist on transferrable AP or IB credit being a key outcome of every high school, and not just of the fortunate, funded few.

Recommendation C: Ensure honors-level course rigor by linking college credit to completion of standardized assessments; in the case of DE courses, grant college credit only if taught by college faculty on college campuses.

Research demonstrates that these ECHS programs, with their absence of standardized assessments combined with little oversight, are not good investments unless the program design intentionally features high school students attending collegiate-level courses on the two- or four-year campus.

This is different from the current practice, where many ECHS programs are located in high school. The lower cost per credit hour of ECHS programs seems attractive, and, as a result, many states have encouraged the proliferation of ECHS programs in the hope of achieving a lower cost-per-degree. However, without being on a college campus, high school students simply do not experience the academic rigor and the social benefits of being immersed in a college course in a manner that ensures their longitudinal success, both in subsequent courses as well as in the completion of their intended degree.

We believe rigorous college-level curricula should be offered to all high school students, either under the auspices of AP and IB or on the two-year or four-year college campus.

Recommendation D: Provide high school students with "academic check-ups," ideally in their junior year, to identify strengths and weaknesses as well as strategies to prepare themselves for college.

Open-access admissions policies telegraph to students that working hard in high school is largely unnecessary. Diploma in hand, any student in America can saunter up to a community college and enroll. There is nothing inherently wrong with this strategy if we think of community colleges as extensions of high school, and if we believe that low retention and completion rates are an acceptable trade-off for open-admission institutions. We do not.

Supporting open admissions means honoring the fact that these institutions have taken on the toughest challenge in higher education. Despite what alumni of elite institutions might tell you, community colleges and other open-access institutions are as much "destinations of choice" as their exceedingly more expensive institutional brethren.

How are we to instill in students the drive that college is a substantive intellectual leap from the comfy confines of their high school? Are there strategies that will communicate to students that preparing well for this transition—regardless of whether they wish to pursue a certificate, associate's degree, or baccalaureate degree—represents the best way to animate their educational dreams?

One option is merely to ask open-access institutions to stop admitting students with mediocre or low high school grades, a slippery slope that would meld these institutions seamlessly with their more selective institutional cousins. Even hardened critics of open-access institutions would likely despair if community colleges exited the higher education landscape.

We believe a better strategy is strengthening relationships among high schools and community colleges by administering low-stakes assessments that provide students with early insight into their capabilities for succeeding in college-level work. These low-stakes assessments should be rapidly followed with targeted strategies to improve their skills.

Suggesting additional testing in K–12 schools is unlikely to be met with much enthusiasm; indeed, it might be viewed with some degree of suspicion. What we advocate, however, is not a summative assessment of a student's aptitude or admission to elite colleges and universities. Rather, it is a recommendation to bolster student readiness for success in any postsecondary institution by providing them with concrete and actionable steps with which to prepare for college.

This is not a radical notion. Many community colleges administer placement exams to high school students to achieve this purpose. In some states, such as Michigan, Idaho, and Colorado, high schools hold school-day administration of college entrance exams such as the SAT and ACT to assess student capabilities for college. For many years, the California State University system asked students to complete a short test as part of California's high school exit exam and then provided students with online courses and workshops to improve skills based on the outcomes of that assessment.

The thrust of this recommendation is to signal strongly to students before they graduate from high school about the kinds of work they will need to accomplish in order to succeed in college. Any assessment must also include the provision of free and effective resources designed to improve their skills.

An external reality check about their postsecondary future frequently proves invaluable.

One could argue that such a reality check is called "high school," and that adding an assessment to the mix simply complicates matters. However, it is one thing for your homeroom teacher to imply that you have a questionable postsecondary future but quite another when a third party, in the form of a standardized assessment, tells you the same thing.

A low-stakes assessment will not prevent students from going to college. But it has the advantage of telegraphing the virtues of preparation to students who need direction and assistance while honoring the community colleges' distinctive academic moniker, and it helps strengthen the bridge between K–12 and community colleges.

Finding 2: Transition and Transfer Are a Fact of Student Postsecondary Life—Deal with It

Historically, transfer referred primarily to the pathway between community colleges and four-year institutions. In the twenty-first century, transfer now encompasses a lifetime of learning in a variety of institutions. It also involves various forms of academic credit, reaching back into the high school with AP and IB credit and ECHS programs, and later including PLA and CBE, and credits earned online.

Although the transfer pathway offers many avenues of opportunity, the fundamental operational inefficiency of transfer from the very beginning has only grown more tangled. Our increasingly complex credit landscape, combined with the shifting demographics of the United States, require a transfer function that truly works for neo-traditional as well as traditional students.

As a nation, we must respond to the challenge of "no credit left behind" with a renewed focus on investments, policies, and practices that foster an effective and efficient transfer function as an educational and moral imperative.

Americans have been on the move for decades—but the portability of their college credit has not. College credits often do not transfer, and stay safely secured at their originating postsecondary institutions. The ubiquity of the Internet means that students in the future will travel even farther, even if they stay put. Educational providers around the globe beckon them on computers and smart phones.

Traditional colleges and universities that make credit transfer easier for their students will reap the reward of future enrollments. Our focus on PLA and CBE recommendations are key to this cry: "If you won't take my credit, will you at least let me demonstrate my competency?"

Recommendation E: Incentivize the use of PLA, sometimes known as CPL or simply learning assessment.

We believe that awarding academic credit for learning earned outside of the classroom should be in place both for traditional undergraduates and for neo-traditional students. The power of PLA could be transformative for the national economy because it encourages, incentivizes, and recognizes life-long learning with the awarding of transferable academic credit.

As described in chapter 5, awarding a minimum of nine credits for academic credit earned outside of the classroom results in graduation rates that are two-and-a-half times higher than for similarly presenting students not receiving PLA. Despite our initial skepticism, these research findings are so compelling that we strongly recommend the comprehensive implementation of PLA on every college campus.

The noble origins of PLA are found in the ACE recommendations for how colleges and universities might best account for the education and training that returning World War II veterans had received in the military. These widely accepted recommendations for the awarding of academic credit capitalized on the nation's investments in service men and women while incentivizing and accelerating degree attainment by current and former military members.

ACE later supplemented these recommendations with the CREDIT initiative in 1974, which expanded the awarding of academic credit for appropriate military training into the civilian arena. These important efforts have been further augmented by the College Board's CLEP exams that also award academic credit for prior learning. Although faculty acceptance is highest for exam-awarded PLA, rigorous portfolio reviews provide another important avenue for prior-learning credit.

We also see the broader implementation and acceptance of PLA as a social justice equity issue. Many institutions are seeking to expand or have expanded the transcription and awarding of academic credit for workplace internships undertaken by their traditional students. Indeed, students and their families frequently see academic credit for internships as a valuable and powerful link between the academy and future employment opportunities.

To be equitable, we should award academic credit for learning outside of the classroom for our traditional undergraduates as well as for our neo-traditional students. Institutions, with the same level of faculty assessment and rigor, should strive to award academic credit earned outside the classroom, whether from the military, homeschooling, volunteer work, or the job experiences of neo-traditional students.

Recommendation F: Refine the use of CBE as a strategy for easing credit-transfer issues between and among postsecondary education institutions.

What is the solution to the credit-transfer problem in an increasingly online educational environment in which a variety of service providers—higher education, corporate, and community-based—will compete for student enrollments? How will we serve "swirling" students who will increasingly generate transcripts from several colleges and universities in search of a coherent degree outcome?

Demonstrating competency—rather than totaling up Carnegie units based on meeting a required number of hours in a classroom—in a fragmented higher education system may be the only way we can bring coherence to a credit-transfer system that has proved problematic for students and institutions. CBE is not the only solution, but it should be one of the solutions, providing students with a nearly unassailable intellectual challenge to higher education.

Although the research is not yet persuasive—partially due to the great variety of the models currently in use—we believe this approach has potential. Mega-universities that utilize CBE as their instructional model, such as Western Governors University (with a 29 percent six-year graduation rate), are making strides at improving the efficacy of CBE.

The most successful CBE models, such as those currently in place in College Unbound (with an 80 percent graduation rate), utilize a mix-modality pedagogical approach that bundles CBE and PLA with online instruction, which is further supplemented with invaluable face-to-face support and community building. Although additional research is needed, the most significant positive benefits currently occur when CBE is combined with other high-impact practices.

Finding 3: Online Learning Is Here to Stay and Must Address the Needs of the Neo-Traditional Student

For those of us old enough to remember, television was to be the great higher education leveler. It never happened. Our skepticism regarding the transformative qualities of online learning are informed by this historical prejudice (and the empirical evidence, but more about that in a minute). We are not Luddites, however.

The necessity of a smartphone to participate in daily living—arranging rides for the kids, managing our calendars, or ordering cat litter—may be unnerving, but it is a fact of modern life. It cannot be surprising, then, that the future of how we engage with postsecondary education will change. More and more students will expect that their learning be moderated by a computer screen and an instructor who might as well be an avatar. The effectiveness of online learning, however, especially for neo-traditional students, is ambiguous at best.

Our recommendations reflect a distrust of nonhuman, unsophisticated, mediated exchange. Still, online education skeptics, especially those like us who were educated in a different, Internet-less epoch, must question our biases. Rather than seeking to minimize or discriminate against the transfer or acceptance of online courses, credentials, and degrees, we should be identifying ways to ensure the highest quality with the most equitable impact for all learners.

Online learning, when further powered with AI and when enhanced with the power of engagement and community found in face-to-face support, goes a long way toward building equitable higher education models.

Recommendation G: Pursue online learning combined with robust AI *and* place-based learning-supports.

As we described in chapter 7, the evidence for the effectiveness of current online course offerings is murky. It is full of qualifications about the extent to which effectiveness is mediated by in-class convenings and its potential (negative) impact on students from underrepresented groups. Online education alone, then, is not a perfect solution, even though it has some benefits, such as its ability to help mitigate the pernicious effects of education deserts, where there are no place-based higher education options within a hundred miles.

Online education outfitted with AI that dynamically adjusts and supports individual student learning would seem to have the best future. As cited in chapter 7, research underwritten by the Gates Foundation demonstrates the positive impact of courses outfitted with AI. Courses employing AI dramatically decrease the rates of DFW (D, Failure, or Withdraw) grades for Pell Grant–eligible and traditionally underrepresented community members when compared to similarly presenting students attending purely online courses.

We also believe that AI-enhanced online education should be further supplemented with "offline channel" face-to-face student support, whether located at traditional postsecondary institutions or at workplace or community locations that might better accommodate the academic and life challenges students face. This mixed-modality, "high tech" approach combined with the "high touch" human support and community hold tremendous promise for positively transforming our educational landscape.

We must also examine our nation's enormous investment in online higher education. Mega-universities, such as Western Governors University, the University of Phoenix, and Southern New Hampshire University, currently enroll nearly one out of every five online students. And the American taxpayer is footing the bill. These universities receive a substantial percentage of their revenue from federal funding via student Pell Grants.

More submerged and murky are the enormous costs to the American taxpayer that result from the corporate partnerships that are so popular at mega-universities. Students are required to complete an application for federal financial aid, frequently resulting in the disbursement of Pell Grant funding.

The company only need pay the remaining tuition dollars. However, those dollars are then refunded to the company, and the American taxpayer subsidizes employer corporate tuition assistance programs via Section 127 of the US tax code.

This portion of the code permits corporate tax write-offs for tuition costs as employee professional development expenses at the rate of up to $5,250 per employee per year. With all of this (sometimes hard to see) funding, might there be more effective ways of investing our federal financial resources in higher education?

In order to work for neo-traditional students, AI-enhanced online education needs to be further supplemented with the recommendations below. We must shift our submerged investments in the corporate/educational realm in a manner that re-directs funds directly to US institutions and that provides all students with the holistic academic and life supports necessary to provide not merely educational access but transformative educational success.

Finding 4: Neo-Traditional Students Represent the Future of American Higher Education; We Either Serve Them or Close Our Doors

Our most startling finding was not simply that the future of higher education would be populated by men and women largely from groups that have little historical connection with college and the language of the academy, but that the shift would be so dramatic. We were warned, of course. In the early 1990s, education pundits predicted a "demographic tidal wave" that would significantly alter the college-going population and perhaps overwhelm higher education institutions.

Higher education's reaction to this tidal wave of students was largely symbolic and a little defensive. (Was our dismay signaled by the use of a natural disaster as an apt metaphor to welcome a new constituency of students to our colleges and universities?) In the past three decades, students from emergent ethnic and racial groups have burst on the higher education scene in extraordinary numbers.

More amazing is the degree to which adult students, especially those with children, and students from low-income groups are entering college. This has been fueled, at least in part, by the elemental idea that if rising economically via postsecondary education was good enough for elites, then it ought to be good for everyone.

Our recommendations for serving neo-traditional students might seem radical: we believe that colleges and universities should offer not just tuition remuneration (as in the various "free college" proposals) but also supports such as textbook stipends, housing allowances, childcare, and food allowances. Some will argue, of course, that higher education has no business providing this degree of social scaffolding and that it is ill-prepared and under-funded to participate in such a sweeping mandate.

Although we are sympathetic to a postsecondary system that has its hands full increasing completion rates among students who are prepared for college, we see this wrap-around model as the best way to propel the new majority of students to degree completion. This is especially true at a time when a recent study of California community college students revealed that nearly half have experienced food insecurity in the past year, 60 percent have experienced housing insecurity, and nearly one in five have experienced homelessness in the past year.[4]

Recommendation H: Ensure students are provided with comprehensive place-based support.

The effectiveness of this support cannot be underestimated. The holistic level of programming is implemented with the full realization that, for many students, academic challenges are only one of the many obstacles they face. Housing and food insecurity, combined with other life challenges, present substantial obstacles for students. In order to foster both access and success, comprehensive levels of support are required.

One of the most effective, research-tested models employing a comprehensive, "whole student" approach is exemplified by the partnership between New York City's Office of the Mayor and CUNY's Accelerated Study in Associates Program (ASAP) as detailed in chapter 9. The ASAP model is further enhanced with CUNY's Single Stop College Initiative, which intentionally connects students to the federal, state, and local benefits they are eligible to receive.

The price for these wrap-around services is high. However, even allowing for the higher cost of instruction and support, because of the dramatic doubling of graduation rates of ASAP students, there is a dramatically lower cost-per-degree awarded, at $6,500 less than the cost per graduate for comparison group students.

The resulting public benefits are huge, with research documenting a whopping return of $3 to $4 for every $1 invested in the ASAP program. These graduates are well-positioned to pay increased taxes on their now-higher income and are also much less likely to require spending on public assistance, public health, and the criminal justice system. Moreover, children of graduates are also much more likely to attend and succeed in college, further extending these longitudinal benefits in an incalculable fashion.

If we truly seek to improve the educational outcomes of our most vulnerable students, this is a model template for how to do it. ASAP-like approaches embody the most compelling aspects of our democratic ideal, where education opportunities are combined with the appropriate level of academic and life supports in a manner that truly ensures both access and success for all members of society.

Recommendation 1: Provide neo-traditional students with families with comprehensive childcare.

America is experiencing a dramatic rise in students balancing the demands of their collegiate academic pursuits with parenting: an astonishing 26 percent of US undergraduates are simultaneously raising children. At community colleges, the percentage is even higher, with about one out of every three students balancing parenthood with their studies. Over half of these individuals face the additional challenge of being a single parent. Only 8 percent of single-mother students graduate with an associate's or bachelor's degree within six years.

Anyone who has raised a child must be sympathetic to the dilemmas parent-students face daily as they navigate multiple, mutually exclusive obligations. It is both a moral and an economic lesson. Moral because no parent will abandon his or her child to complete a postsecondary degree, although that is what we ask them to do when childcare is unavailable. And economic because parents with a postsecondary degree or credential are far more able to provide for themselves and their family with an income that sustains a family and contributes to the community.

Notable institutions are harnessing the motivation and desire of parent-students to provide for their family's future, including College Unbound and Los Angeles Valley College. At College Unbound, which was founded to meet the needs of neo-traditional students, the graduation rate is an impressive 80 percent, and every class meeting offers both free food and free childcare.

Los Angeles Valley College has taken this approach even further with its impressive Family Resource Center, which includes a wide array of supports such as academic counseling and tutoring, after-school (school-age) childcare, a lactation room with a refrigerator for breast milk, a kid-friendly study lounge, textbook assistance, computer and printing access, school supplies, a children's clothing exchange, organic produce, diapers/wipes/formula, and more.

A comprehensive parent-student approach means that the center's staff includes a marriage/family therapist and a social worker. These broad, family-focused, strategic, and intentional investments provide remarkable returns in the long run. Research demonstrates that, for every dollar a single mother invests in college, she gets $16.50 back over her lifetime after earning her associate's degree.

Not even counting the reductions in public assistance, which run into the hundreds of millions of dollars, there are significant resulting tax contributions of nearly $8 billion over the lifetime of all the single mothers expected to graduate with a degree. What could be more dramatic, transformative, and democratic for American higher education than for us to fully and appropriately support our parent-students, thus transforming both their lives and that of their families? And all this at a lower cost-per-degree for the American taxpayer, too.

Finding 5: Getting Ahead Means Getting a Job— Lifelong Learning Is Survival for Neo-Traditional Students and for Postsecondary Education

We—the authors of this book—are deeply thankful for the opportunity to have benefitted from a traditional higher education experience. Our pathways meant earning bachelor's degrees and graduate degrees at brick and mortar institutions, then sticking around to become part of the faculty and the administration. Although the American economy has ebbed and flowed during our college-going years, and concern about jobs was an important consideration in the degrees we pursued, it was not our only consideration.

Today, however, the neo-traditional student believes she has fewer degrees of freedom. In the midst of an income gap, the largest the nation has seen since the Gilded Age, fears about employment often dominate conversations about the value of college.

Throughout this book, we unabashedly recommend that students earn at least a baccalaureate degree as a sound strategy against a roiling economic landscape. Still, the key realization for us is that the liberal arts—within the context of open-access institutions—is best enhanced when students are connected with real-world credentials that have work-place meaning and the ability to earn a family-sustaining job.

Recommendation J: Build curricula that begins the student's postsecondary pathway with labor-value credentials and provides avenues for on-going learning and eventual transfer.

To meet the needs of neo-traditional students, US institutions should consider a broad and sweeping curricular redesign that emulates the success of Brigham Young University's PathwayConnect. The most powerful and replicable component of the PathwayConnect program is its "certificate first" curricular strategy combined with a no-credit-left-behind ideology and ethos. Retention and graduation data clearly indicate that PathwayConnect's flipped-model curricular innovation results in powerful gains for the most at-risk students. It also improves job prospects and earning potential from the very start and helps to avoid the miserable combination of earning some college credits, accumulating student debt, and yet failing to earn a transformative degree or certificate.

Recommendation K: Foster educational partnerships that connect the academy with corporate and nonprofit partnerships.

Our national educational policies should encourage corporate partnerships that ensure academic learning, whether provided online or face-to-face, is supplemented with place-based support. Rather than replicating the ASU/Starbucks model, where the federal government provides the bulk of the tuition dollars for online education via Pell Grants and the corporation funds the remaining balance (which the federal government quietly refunds to the corporation through employee-development tax write-offs), these workplace partnerships ideally would replicate the College Unbound model.

In that model, employees gather onsite after work to develop a deeper understanding of the academic material delivered online and to foster the sense of community and support vital to their success and graduation. Free childcare and meals are provided during every class meeting in remarkable support for parent-students and their families.

Building intentional corporate partnerships would help fill the gaps of American education deserts (where no college or university is located within a hundred miles) by providing new educational sites. The companies benefit via higher levels of employee retention and securing their own educated workforce. For neo-traditional students, workplace-based learning is evaluated and included in valuable stackable credentials that lead to degrees in a manner similar to our transcription of academic credit for the paid and unpaid internships of traditional undergraduate students.

CLOSING THOUGHTS

These findings and recommendations make clear our conviction that US investments in higher education must focus on providing the holistic academic and life supports required to foster student success and graduation. The initial cost of these investments will be higher. But the resulting lower cost-per-degree translates into transformative gains for individuals and for society.

Ensuring the success of both traditional and neo-traditional students as they enter and successfully navigate college through graduation will translate into higher academic credential and degree attainment rates. More students from all strata of US society will be rewarded with postsecondary degrees and credentials. Argue, if you must, whether these credentials represent an authentic upskilling of individuals' readiness for work or simply reflect the inexorable economic outcome of employers wanting to benefit from higher education rates of potential workers.

For us, that debate, while legitimate, is less central if the credentials and degrees our institutions award are rigorous and relevant. What we know for certain is that the investment *we now make* helps produce a cadre of students with scattered or unusable credits, no credential, and student loan debt—a cadre of students without the resources to overcome these outcomes.

In a society in which elites will bribe others to gain entry to the nation's most highly ranked colleges and universities, it is only quaint to debate the question *if* a postsecondary degree has value. The answer to that question is hardly a state secret. What is essential is not the "if" but the "how."

In the twenty-first century, there is mounting concern that our future sees less opportunity for individuals to participate in the middle class by qualifying for a family-sustaining job or to benefit intellectually and culturally from the mind-expanding virtues of a liberal arts education. Our response, then, is to insist on strategic investments that provide the far-ranging impacts of degree attainment for all Americans.

Nothing could be more transformative for our country than to live up to the highest levels of our democracy's aspirations and to provide both the access to higher education and the support to attain a degree to all citizens ready and willing to work to improve their lives. What those investments must be are the heart of this book. Although our recommendations for higher education's future involve the kind of risk inherent to such informed prognostications, we can, at least, be certain and strategic about our educational yearnings.

Notes

PREFACE

1. Douglas T. Shapiro, "Student Transfer and Mobility: Pathways, Scale, and Outcomes for Student Success," in *Building Transfer Student Pathways for College and Career Success*, eds. Mark Allen Poisel and Sonya Joseph (Columbia, SC: University of South Carolina, National Resource Center for the First Year Experience and Students in Transition and the National Institute for the Study of Transfer Students, 2019), p. 3.

2. College Board, *Winning the Skills Race and Strengthening the Middle-Class: An Action Agenda for Community Colleges* (New York, NY: College Board, 2008).

3. Suzanne Mettler, *From Soldiers to Citizens: The G. I. Bill and the Making of the Greatest Generation* (New York, NY: Oxford University Press, 2005), pp. 166–67.

4. Ta-Nehisi Coates, "Making the Case for Reparations," *Atlantic Magazine*, June 2014, www.theatlantic.com/magazine/archive/2014/06/the-case-for-reparations/361631/.

CHAPTER 1

1. Mike Rose, *Back to School: Why Everyone Deserves a Second Chance at Education* (New York, NY: The New Press, 2012), p. 143.

2. Manuel N. Gomez, *College for the Community: Academic Cultures and Institutional Change* (Paper Presented at the American Association of Higher Education National Conference on Higher Education, March 20, 1999), p. 1.

3. Kevin J. Dougherty, *The Contradictory College: The Conflicting Origins, Impacts, and Futures of the Community College* (Albany, NY: State University of New York Press, 1994).

4. Ibid., 261. Sarah Goldrick-Rab makes a similar point by linking transition issues to a larger body of work in the K–12 sector, where student transfer from one institution to another has been clearly documented as a drag on educational attainment: "Another barrier to academic momentum . . . is the requirement that community college students move to another institution to earn a bachelor's degree. . . . Studies of student mobility in elementary and secondary education in the US indicate that mobile students, especially those from disadvantaged backgrounds have difficulty coping with moves to new schools, often suffering psychologically, socially, and academically" (S. Goldrick-Rab, *Promoting Academic Momentum at Community Colleges: Challenges and Opportunities* [New York, NY: Community College Research Center, Teachers College, Columbia University, 2007], p. 14).

5. Steven Brint and Jerome Karabel, *The Diverted Dream: Community Colleges and the Promise of Educational Opportunity in America, 1900–1985* (New York, NY: Oxford University Press, 1989).

6. Richard C. Richardson, Jr. and Lewis W. Bender, *Fostering Minority Access and Achievement in Higher Education* (San Francisco, CA: Jossey-Bass, 1987), p. 22.

7. J. R. Cole, *The Great American University: Its Rise to Prominence; Its Indispensable National Role: Why It Must Be Protected* (New York, NY: Public Affairs, 2009).

8. American Association of Community Colleges, *Fast Facts, 2018* (Washington, DC: AACC, 2018), www.aacc.nche.edu/research-trends/fast-facts/.

9. S. Trainor, "How Community Colleges Changed the Whole Idea of Education in America," *Time*, October 20, 2015, http://time.com/4078143/community-college-history/.

10. Dougherty, *The Contradictory College.*

11. S. J. Handel and R. A. Williams, *The Promise of the Transfer Pathway* (New York, NY: College Board, 2012).

12. William Eells, *Present Status of Junior College Terminal Education* (Washington, DC: American Association of Junior Colleges, 1941), p. 17. Eells telegraphed the long-term strategy of community colleges a decade earlier by noting, drolly, that "The junior college is succeeding in the first step of its preparatory function, namely in giving its students an ambition to go on to further work in the university. . . . [T]here are many reasons to suppose that it is succeeding too well" (quoted in Brint and Karabel, *The Diverted Dream*, 43).

13. "Bridging the Higher Education Divide: Strengthening Community Colleges and Restoring the American Dream," *Report of the Century Foundation Task Force on Preventing Community Colleges from Becoming Separate and Unequal* (New York, NY: Century Foundation Press, 2013).

14. US Government Accountability Office, *Higher Education: Students Need More Information to Help Reduce Challenges in Transferring College Credits*, GAO 17-574 (Washington, DC: GAO, August 2017).

15. State Higher Education Executive Officers Association, *State Higher Education Finance* (Boulder, CO: SHEEO, 2019), www.sheeo.org/.

16. College Board, *Trends in Higher Education* (New York, NY: College Board, 2018); College Board, *Trends in College Pricing* (New York, NY: College Board, 2017).

17. Cole, *The Great American University*.

18. W. Zumeta, D. W. Breneman, P. M. Callan, and J. E. Finney, *Financing American Higher Education in the Era of Globalization* (Cambridge, MA: Harvard Educational Press, 2012).

19. Andrew S. Rosen, *Change.edu: Rebooting for the New Talent Economy* (New York, NY: Kaplan Publishing, 2011), pp. 79–80.

20. Ibid., 94.

CHAPTER 2

1. William Rainey Harper, *The Prospects of the Small College* (Chicago, IL: University of Chicago Press, 1901), p. 26, https://books.google.com.

2. Brint and Karabel, *The Diverted Dream*.

3. Dougherty, *The Contradictory College*.

4. J. M. Beach, *Gateway to Opportunity? A History of the Community College in the United States* (Sterling, VA: Stylus Press, 2010).

5. Arthur M. Cohen and Florence B. Brawer, *The American Community College*, 5th edition (San Francisco, CA: Jossey-Bass, 2008).

6. Ibid.

7. Beach, *Gateway to Opportunity?*

8. William Rainey Harper, *The Trend in Higher Education* (Chicago, IL: University of Chicago Press, 1905), pp. 9, 19.

9. Harper writes: "I use the name 'junior college,' for lack of a better term, to cover the work of the freshman and sophomore years" (Ibid., 378). For this chapter, we will privilege Harper's term for these colleges in keeping with the backward glance of this treatment, fully appreciating that "community college" is the widely accepted, modern moniker of these institutions and a more comprehensive description of their wide-ranging mission.

10. Ibid., 347–48.

11. Ibid., 7–8.

12. Brint and Karabel, *The Diverted Dream*.

13. Harper, *Trend in Higher Education*, 363.

14. Ibid., 374–75: "[A]fter all, the greatest difficulty of the small college is its lack of means with which to do the work demanded in these days of modern methods, the methods of the library and the laboratory. . . . The cost per capita of instruction furnished the high school students in some of our cities, even where the classes are crowded, exceeds the average cost per capita of instruction furnished in many of our colleges. The demands of modern methods have quadrupled the difficulty in this respect. . . . With the introduction of laboratory work in the various sciences the expenditures required for laboratories and for equipment are very great. Without money these demands cannot be met, and yet without meeting the demands of the

present age our colleges all over the land are graduating students who are impressed with the belief that they have been educated in accordance with modern ideas."

15. Ibid., 154.

16. Harper did not originate this view. Cohen and Brawer note that leaders of several major universities in the 1850s and 1860s believed that US universities would never emerge as authentic research centers until they eliminated the lower division from the curriculum (*American Community College*, 7).

17. "The modern high school, sometimes called the 'people's college,' is a development of twenty-five years. Much of the work formerly done by the colleges is now being done by the high schools. . . . There is no evidence that the public attitude toward the high school will change. If there were no other reason for the support of the high school by the public, reason enough would be found in the fact that without such work it would be impossible to provide teachers for the lower schools" (Harper, *Trend in Higher Education*, 363). See also William Rainey Harper, *The Prospects of the Small College* (Chicago, IL: University of Chicago Press, 1900), https://books.google.com.

18. Harper, *Trend in Higher Education*, 359.

19. American Association of Community Colleges, *Fast Facts* (Washington, DC: AACC, 2019), www.aacc.nche.edu/research-trends/fast-facts/.

20. Dougherty, *The Contradictory College*, 23.

21. This unresolved elitism remains problematic to this day. Four-year colleges profess a great desire to increase the racial and ethnic diversity of their incoming students. Look at the mission statement of most institutions: the desire to increase the representation of students from under-resourced groups is almost always mentioned as a major goal. Given the diversity of most community colleges, it is hard to square this with the lack of interest in transfer students.

22. Harper, *The Prospect of the Small College*, 41–42. Harper believed that the organization of junior colleges and research institutions would be bound together through professional associations. These associations would be especially productive because of the clear missions of both segments of higher education. He writes: "With better classifications of educational work, with the greater similarity of standards for admissions and for graduation, and with the variety of type secured, so that individual institutions will have individual responsibilities, there will be found a basis for cooperation such as has not hitherto existed. . . . It will secure results which no institution of its own strength could secure. *It will lift educational work above the petty jealousies and rivalries which today bring reproach and disgrace upon it*" (Harper, *Prospects of the Small College*, 41–42, emphasis added).

23. US Government Accountability Office, *Higher Education*, www.gao.gov/assets/690/686530.pdf.

24. A. W. Logue, *Pathways to Reform: Credits and Conflicts at the City University of New York* (Princeton, NJ: Princeton University Press, 2017).

25. Harper, *Trend in Higher Education*, 371.

26. S. J. Handel, "Community College Students Earning the Baccalaureate: The Good News Could Be Better," *College and University* 89, no. 2 (2018): 22–30.

27. Dougherty, *The Contradictory College*, 67–68.

28. B. R. Clark, "The 'Cooling Out' Function in Higher Education," *American Journal of Sociology* 65, no. 6 (May 1960): 569–76.

29. National Center for Education Statistics, *120 Years of American Education: A Statistical Portrait*, ed. Thomas E. Snyder (Washington, DC: US Department of Education, 1993), table 8, p. 34, https://nces.ed.gov/pubs93/93442.pdf.

30. Cole, *The Great American University*.

31. Jessica Dickler, "Free Community College Is Nearly a Reality in 20 States," *CNBC*, December 2018, www.cnbc.com/2018/12/14/free-college-is-now-a-reality-in-nearly-20-states.html.

32. James E. Rosenbaum, Caitlin E. Ahearn, and Janet E. Rosenbaum, *Bridging the Gaps: College Pathways to Career Success* (New York, NY: Russell Sage Foundation, 2017).

33. Harper, *Prospects of the Small College*, 40, https://books.google.com.

CHAPTER 3

1. Robert Zemsky, *Making Reform Work: The Case for Transforming American Higher Education* (New Brunswick, NJ: Rutgers University Press, 2009), p. 196.

2. American Association of Community Colleges, *Fast Facts*, 2019, www.aacc.org.

3. See B. Weiner, "Attribution Theory," *International Encyclopedia of Education* 6 (2010): 558–63; B. Weiner, "The Attributional Approach to Emotion and Motivation: History, Hypotheses, Home Runs, and Headaches/Heartaches," *Emotion Review* 6, no. 4 (2014): 558–63.

4. See Angela Duckworth, *Grit: The Power of Passion and Perseverance* (New York, NY: Scribner, 2016); Carol S. Dweck, *Mindsets: The New Psychology of Success* (New York, NY: Ballantine Books, 2016).

5. Janell Ross, "Is Open-Access Community College a Bad Idea?" *The Atlantic*, June 23, 2014, https://www.theatlantic.com/politics/archive/2014/06/is-open-access-community-college-a-bad-idea/431052/.

6. Gallup, Inc., *2016 Gallup Student Poll: A Snapshot of Results and Findings*, 2017, www.sac.edu/research/PublishingImages/Pages/research-studies/. See also R. Breneman, "Gallup Student Poll Finds Engagement in School Dropping by Grade Level," *Education Week*, March 22, 2016, www.edweek.org/ew/articles/2016/03/23/gallup-student-poll-finds-engagement-in-school.html.

7. M. W. Kirst and A. Venezia, *From High School to College: Improving Opportunities for Success in Postsecondary Education* (San Francisco, CA: Jossey Bass, 2004), p. 8.

8. J. Rosenbaum, *Beyond College for All: Career Paths for the Forgotten Half* (New York, NY: Russell Sage Foundation, 2001).

9. The percentages are greater for *non-college-bound* students. See Ibid., 61.

10. Ibid., 68, 61.

11. Kirst and Venezia, *From High School to College*, 296.

12. Ibid., 278–79.

13. For a literature review, see S. J. Handel, "Community College Students Earning the Baccalaureate: The Good News Could Be Better," *College and University* 89, no. 2 (2013): 22–30.

14. William G. Bowen, Matthew M. Chingos, and Michael S. McPherson, *Crossing the Finishing Line: Completing College at America's Public Universities* (Princeton, NJ: Princeton University Press, 2009), p. 143.

15. Handel, "Community College Students," 28.

16. Michael McGarrah and Steven Hurlburt, *The Shifting Academic Workforce: Where Are the Contingent Faculty?* (Washington, DC: American Institutes for Research and Delta Cost Project, 2016), www.air.org/sites/default/files/downloads/report/Shifting-Academic-Workforce-November-2016.pdf.

17. Center for Community College Student Engagement, *Show Me the Way: The Power of Advising in Community Colleges* (Austin, TX: University of Texas at Austin, College of Education, Department of Educational Leadership and Policy, Program in Higher Education Leadership, 2018), www.ccsse.org/nr2018/Show_Me_Way.pdf.

18. American Association of Community Colleges, *Fast Facts*. Note that, throughout this book, we are following IPEDS definitions for data reporting on ethnic categories (thus: American Indian, not Native American).

19. Kirst and Venezia, *From High School to College*, 289–91.

CHAPTER 4

1. Mortimer J. Adler, *Reforming Education: The Opening of the American Mind* (New York, NY: Macmillan, 1977), p. 111.

2. College Board, *College Credit in High School: Working Group Report* (New York, NY: College Board, 2017), pp. 8–9, https://secure-media.collegeboard.org/pdf/research/college-credit-high-school-working-group-report.pdf.

3. Chester E. Finn, Jr. and Andrew E. Scanlan, *Learning in the Fast Lane: The Past, Present, and Future of Advanced Placement* (Princeton, NJ: Princeton University Press, 2019), p. 32.

4. Ibid., 40.

5. Ibid., 41.

6. Ibid., 44.

7. Nat Malkus, *AP at Scale: Public School Students in Advanced Placement, 1990–2013* (American Enterprise Institute for Public Policy Research, 2015), p. 4, https://www.aei.org/research-products/report/ap-at-scale-public-school-students-in-advanced-placement-1990-2013/.

8. Nat Malkus, *The AP Peak: Public Schools Offering Advanced Placement, 2000–2012* (Washington, DC: American Enterprise Institute for Public Policy Research), p. 4, https://www.heartland.org/_template-assets/documents/publications/aei_-_2016-01-14_ap_at_peak_-_public_schools_offering_advanced_placement_2000-12.pdf.

9. College Board, *Class of 2018 AP Data Overview* (New York, NY: College Board), p. 2, https://reports.collegeboard.org/ap-program-results/class-2018-data.

10. Finn and Scanlan, *Learning in the Fast Lane*, 41.

11. Erik Gilbert, "How Dual Enrollment Contributes to Inequality," *Chronicle of Higher Education* 64, no. 11 (2017).

12. Hanover Research, *Best Practices for AP Programs* (Washington, DC: Hanover Research, September 2014), p. 11, www.ncappartnership.org/uploads/3/9/7/4/39749470/best-practices-for-ap-programs.pdf.

13. Ibid., 11.

14. "Grant Lets All Dallas ISD High Schoolers Earn $100 per AP Test Passed," *Dallas Morning News*, September 20, 2010, www.dallasnews.com/news/education/2010/09/20/grant-lets-all-dallas-isd-high-schoolers-earn-100-per-ap-test-passed/.

15. Ibid.

16. Ibid.

17. Ibid.

18. "The Road to Equity: Expanding AP Access and Success for African-American Students," *Report of the Eli and Edythe Broad Foundation*, Los Angeles, CA, June 2013, www.issuelab.org/resources/15409/15409.pdf.

19. Hanover Research, *Best Practices for AP Programs*, 12.

20. J. Kim and D. D. Bragg, "The Impact of Dual and Articulated Credit on College Readiness and Retention in Four Community Colleges," *Career and Technical Education Research* 33, no. 2 (2008): 133–58.

21. College Board, *College Credit in High School*, 7.

22. Victor M. H. Borden, Jason L. Taylor, Eunkyoung Park, and David J. Seiler, *Dual Credit in U.S. Higher Education: A Study of State Policy and Quality Assurance Practices* (Chicago, IL: Higher Learning Commission, 2013), p. 2, www.hlcommission.org/Publications/dual-credit-programs-and-courses.html.

23. College Board, *College Credit in High School*, 8.

24. John Fink, Davis Jenkins, and Takeshi Yanagiura, *What Happens to Students Who Take Community College 'Dual Enrollment' Courses in High School?* (New York, NY: Community College Research Center, Teachers College, Columbia University, 2017), https://ccrc.tc.columbia.edu/publications/what-happens-community-college-dual-enrollment-students.html.

25. Ibid.

26. Cecilia Speroni, *Determinants of Students' Success: The Role of Advanced Placement and Dual Enrollment Programs* (New York, NY: Community College Research Center, Teachers College, Columbia University, 2011), https://ccrc.tc.columbia.edu/publications/role-advanced-placement-dual-enrollment.html.

27. Ibid.

28. Ibid.

29. Education Commission of the States, *50 State Comparison. Advanced Placement: State Financial Support for AP Course Offerings/AP Success* (Denver, CO: ECS, 2019), http://ecs.force.com/mbdata/MBQuestRT?Rep=AP0216.

30. Ibid.

31. For further details on the IB program, go to www.ibo.org/about-the-ib/.

32. V. Coca, D. Johnson, and T. Kelley-Kemple, *Working to My Potential: The Postsecondary Experiences of CPS Students in the International Baccalaureate Diploma Program* (Chicago, IL: University of Chicago Consortium on Chicago School Research, 2011), p. 9.

33. Ibid., 4.

34. David Steiner and Ashley Berner, "Chicago's Use of the International Baccalaureate: An Education Success Story That Didn't Travel," *Policy Brief from the Johns Hopkins School of Education Institute for Education Policy*, p. 5, https://edpolicy.education.jhu.edu/wp-content/uploads/2015/10/Chicagobaccalaureatemas theadFINAL.pdf.

35. Ibid., 6.

CHAPTER 5

1. Matthew Crawford, *Shop Class as Soulcraft: An Inquiry Into the Value of Work* (New York, NY: Penguin Books, 2009), p. 162.

2. American Council on Education, *The Military Guide* [a website of resources (including videos) for formal courses and occupations offered by all branches of the military] (Washington, DC: ACE, 2019), www.acenet.edu/news-room/Pages/How-to-use-the-Military-Guide.aspx.

3. Mikyung Ryu, *Credit for Prior Learning: From the Student, Campus, and Industry Perspectives* (Washington, DC: ACE Center for Policy Research and Strategy, November 2013), p. 4.

4. D. Shapiro, M. Ryu, F. Huie, and Q. Liu, *Some College, No Degree: A 2019 Snapshot for the Nation and 50 States*, Signature Report No. 17 (Herndon, VA: National Student Clearinghouse Research Center, October 2019), https://nscresearchc enter.org/wp-content/uploads/SCND_Report_2019.pdf.

5. Ryu, *Credit for Prior Learning*, 1.

6. R. Klein-Collins, *Fueling the Race to Postsecondary Success: A 48-Institution Study of Prior Learning Assessment and Adult Student Outcomes* (Chicago, IL: Council for Adult and Experiential Learning, 2010), www.cael.org/pdfs/PLA _Fueling-the-Race.

7. Ibid.

8. Ryu, *Credit for Prior Learning*, 7.

9. Ibid.

10. Ibid., 12.

11. Tennessee Prior Learning Assessment Task Force, *Recommended Standards in Prior Learning Assessment (PLA) Policy and Practice for Tennessee Public Colleges and Universities* (Nashville, TN: TPLATF, August 7, 2012), p. 1.

12. Rebecca Klein-Collins and Kylie Oulahan, *State System PLA Adoption: Lessons from a Three-System Initiative* (Chicago, IL: The Council for Adult an Experiential Learning [CAEL] in Partnership with Montana University System, Ohio Department of Higher Education and Texas A&M University System, 2015).

13. Paul Fain, "College Credit Without College," *Inside Higher Ed*, May 7, 2012.

14. Matt Bergman, "Four Reasons Your Campus Should Be Offering Prior Learning Assessment Credit," *EvoLLLution*, November 6, 2019, https://evolllution.com/programming/applied-and-experiential-learning/the-four-reasons-your-campus-should-be-offering-prior-learning-assessment-credit/.

15. Anthony P. Carnevale, Nicole Smith, and Jeff Strohl, *Help Wanted: Projections of Jobs and Education Requirements Through 2018* (Washington, DC: Georgetown University Center on Education and the Workforce, 2010), p. 17.

16. Daniel Pianko and Carol D'Amico, "Will Big Brands Disrupt Higher Education?" *TechCrunch*, August 28, 2018, https://techcrunch.com/2018/08/28/will-big-brands-disrupt-higher-education/.

17. Quoted in Fain, "College Credit without College."

18. *PLA with a Purpose: Prior Learning Assessment & Ohio's College Completion Agenda* (Columbus, OH: Ohio Board of Regents, University System of Ohio, 2014).

19. Eileen Strempel, "Fostering a Transfer Student Receptive Ecosystem," *Planning for Higher Education Journal* 41, no. 4 (July 2013): 12–17.

CHAPTER 6

1. Jamie Merisotis, *America Needs Talent: Attracting, Educating and Deploying the 21st-Century Workforce* (New York, NY: Rosetta Books, 2015), pp. 83–84.

2. Stephanie Malia Krauss, "How Competency-Based Education May Help Reduce Our Nation's Toughest Inequalities," *Lumina Issue Papers*, 2017. Figures on the number of CBE programs in the United States were reported to the Lumina Foundation by Michael Offerman. In August 2015, Public Agenda conducted the first-ever national survey of CBE programs and reported updated numbers in its survey brief, *A Research Brief on the Survey of Shared Design Elements & Emerging Practices of Competency-Based Education Programs* (Brooklyn, NY: Public Agenda, 2015).

3. Pamela Tate and Rebecca Klein-Collins, *PLA and CBE on the Competency Continuum: The Relationship Between Prior Learning Assessment and Competency Based Education* (Chicago, IL: Council for Adult and Experiential Learning, 2015).

4. Competency-Based Education Network, *Quality Principles and Standards for Competency-Based Education Programs*, Report (Franklin, TN: C-BEN, 2017), www.cbenetwork.org/sites/457/uploaded/files/CBE17__Quality_Standards_FINAL.pdf.

5. "Competency-Based Education Network Announces New Cohort of Member Institutions," *Press Release* (Franklin, TN: C-BEN, 2018), www.cbenetwork.org/wp-content/uploads/2018/09/CBEN_Announces_New_Members.pdf.

6. Mathew W. Lewis, Rick Eden, Chandra Garber, Mollie Rudnick, Lucrecia Santibañez, and Tiffany Tsai, *Equity in Competency Education: Realizing the Potential, Overcoming the Obstacles*, Competency Education Research Series (Boston, MA: Rand Education and Jobs for the Future, 2014).

7. Krauss, "How Competency-Based Education," 12.

8. Andrew P. Kelly and Rooney Columbus, *Innovate and Evaluate: Expanding the Research Base for Competency-Based Education*, American Enterprise Institute Series on Competency-Based Higher Education (Washington, DC: AEI, 2016), p. 2.

9. Katie Larsen McClarty and Matthew N. Gaertner, *Measuring Mastery: Best Practices for Assessment of Competency-Based Education*, American Enterprise Institute Series on Competency-Based Higher Education (Washington, DC: AEI, April 2015), p. 8, www.aei.org/research-products/measuring-mastery-best-practices -for-assessment-in-competency-based-education/.

10. Johann N. Neem, "Experience Matters: Why Competency-Based Education Will Not Replace Seat Time," *Liberal Education*, Fall 2013: 3, www.aacu.org/publica tions-research/periodicals/experience-matters-why-competency-based-education-will -not-replace/.

11. Quoted in Anya Kamenetz, "Are You Competent? Prove It," *New York Times*, October 29, 2013.

CHAPTER 7

1. Marcus Aurelius, *Meditations*, trans. Maxwell Staniforth (New York, NY: Penguin Books, 1964), chap. 12, sec. 20, p. 183.

2. Julie E Seaman, I. Elaine Allen, and Jeff Seaman, *Grade Increase: Tracking Distance Education in the United States* (Oakland, CA: Babson Survey Research Group, 2018), www.onlinelearningsurvey.com/highered.html.

3. National Center for Education Statistics, "Glossary Results: Distance Education," *2019–20 Survey Materials*, https://surveys.nces.ed.gov/ipeds/VisGlossar yAll.aspx.

4. I. Elaine Allen and Jeff Seaman with Russell Poulin and Terri Taylor Straut, *Online Report Card: Tracking Online Education in the United States* (Oakland, CA: Babson Survey Research Group and Quahog Research Group, 2016), https://files.eric .ed.gov/fulltext/ED572777.pdf.

5. Blended learning is "Online activity . . . mixed with classroom meetings, replacing a significant percentage, but not all required face-to-face instructional activities" (Online Learning Consortium: http://onlinelearningconsortium.org/upda ted-e-learning-definitions-2/). "Blended" and "distance" learning definitions are still evolving and are inconsistent at this time across the US higher-education institutions.

6. Allen et al., *Online Report Card*.

7. Ibid.

8. Ibid.

9. Sean Gallagher, "The Beginning of a New Era in the Online Degree Market," *Ed Surge News*, October 31, 2018, www.edsurge.com/news/2018-10-30-the-begi nning-of-a-new-era-in-the-online-degree-market.

10. John Hanc, "Life Is Complicated: Distance Learning Helps," *New York Times*, November 1, 2018, www.nytimes.com/2018/11/01/education/learning/life-is-compli cated-distance-learning-helps.html.

11. Quoted in Ibid.

12. Doug Shapiro and Afet Dunbar, *Completing College: A National View of Student Attainment Rates, Fall 2009 Cohort* (Herndon, VA: National Student Clearinghouse Research Center, November 2015), https://nscresearchcenter.org/wp -content/uploads/SignatureReport10.pdf.

13. Allison Bailey, Nithya Vaduganathan, Tyce Henry, Renee Laverdiere, and Lou Pugliese, *Making Digital Learning Work: Success Strategies from Six Leading Universities and Community Colleges* (Boston, MA: The Boston Consulting Group, March 2018), p. 12, https://edplus.asu.edu/sites/default/files/BCG-Making-Digital-Learning-Work-Apr-2018%20.pdf.

14. Ibid., 22–23.

15. "Deliberate Innovation, Lifetime Education," *Final Report from the Georgia Tech Commission on Creating the Next in Education*, April 2018, www.provost.gatech.edu/cne-home.

16. Sean Gallagher, "How Amazon's Purchase of Whole Foods Highlights the Hybrid, 'Omnichannel' Future of Higher Ed," *Edsurge News*, June 22, 2017, www.edsurge.com/news/2017-06-22-how-amazon-s-purchase-of-whole-foods-highlights-the-hybrid-omnichannel-future-of-higher-ed.

17. Arthur C. Graesser, Mark W. Conley, and Andrew Olney, "Intelligent Tutoring Systems," in *APA Educational Psychology Handbook, Vol. 3: Application to Learning and Teaching*, eds. Karen R. Harris, Steve Graham, and Tim Urdan (Washington, DC: American Psychological Association, 2012).

18. Bailey et al., *Making Digital Learning Work*, 23.

19. Gallagher, "How Amazon's Purchase."

20. David Brooks, "Students Learn from People They Love: Putting Relationship Quality at the Center of Education," *New York Times*, January 17, 2019, www.nytimes.com/2019/01/17/opinion/learning-emotion-education.html.

21. Learning House, *Online College Students 2017: Comprehensive Data on Demands and Preferences* (Louisville, KY: Wiley Education Services, June 24, 2017), www.learninghouse.com/knowledge-center/research-reports/ocs2017/.

22. National Center for Education Statistics, "College Navigator," *Information on Southern New Hampshire University*, https://nces.ed.gov/collegenavigator/?q=southern+new+hampshire&s=all&id=183026.

23. Goldie Blumenstyk, "Meet the New Mega-University: Can the Fast-Growing Southern New Hampshire U. Transform Higher Education?" *Chronicle of Higher Education*, November 11, 2018, www.chronicle.com/article/Meet-the-New-Mega-University/245049.

24. Caitlin Crowe, "Arizona State Will Give Uber Drivers in 8 Cities Free Tuition in Its Online Program," *Chronicle of Higher Education*, November 1, 2018, www.chronicle.com/article/Arizona-State-Will-Give-Uber/244977.

25. See *U.S. Code 127, Educational Assistance Programs*, at www.law.cornell.edu/uscode/text/26/127; Nicholas Turner, "Office of Tax Analysis Working Paper 113, Tax Expenditures for Higher Education," *U.S. Department of the Treasury*, November 2016, p. 16.

26. Susan Adams, "This Company Could Be Your Next Teacher: Coursera Plots a Massive Future for Online Education," *Forbes*, October 16, 2018, www.forbes.com/sites/susanadams/2018/10/16/this-company-could-be-your-next-teacher-coursera-plots-a-massive-future-for-online-education.

27. Doug Lederman, "Who Is Studying Online (and Where)," *Inside Higher Ed*, January 5, 2018, www.insidehighered.com/digital-learning/article/2018/01/05/new-us-data-show-continued-growth-college-students-studying.

28. Nicholas Hillman and Taylor Weichman, *Education Deserts: The Continued Significance of "Place" in the Twenty-First Century. Viewpoints: Voices from the Field* (Washington, DC: American Council on Education, 2016), p. 4.

29. Calvin D. Fogle and Devonda Elliott, "The Market Value of Online Degrees as a Credible Credential," *Global Education Journal* 3 (2013): 1.

30. Ibid., 24.

31. Ben Myers, "Who Lives in Higher Education Deserts: More People Than You Think," *Chronicle of Higher Education*, July 17, 2018.

32. Ibid.

CHAPTER 8

1. Century Foundation, *Bridging the Higher Education Divide: Strengthening Community Colleges and Restoring the American Dream* (New York, NY: Century Foundation Press, 2013), p. 13.

2. Bridget Terry Long, "The Financial Crisis and College Enrollment: How Have Students and Their Families Responded?" in *How the Financial Crisis and Great Recession Affected Higher Education (National Bureau of Economic Research Conference Report)*, eds. Jeffrey R. Brown and Caroline M. Hoxby (Chicago, IL: Chicago University Press, 2015), p. 209.

3. Ibid., 223.

4. Richard Hofstadter, *Anti-Intellectualism in American Life* (New York, NY: Vintage Books, 1962), p. 301.

5. Julian Wyllie, "Why Are States Spending Less on Higher-Ed? Medicaid and Lazy Rivers Could Be to Blame," *Chronicle of Higher Education*, May 1, 2018, www .chronicle.com/article/Why-Are-States-Spending-Less/243281.

6. Douglas Webber, "Higher Ed, Lower Spending: As States Cut Back, Where Has the Money Gone?" *Education Next* 18, no. 3 (Summer 2018), www.educationne xt.org/higher-ed-lower-spending-as-states-cut-back-where-has-money-gone/.

7. Anna Brown, *Most Americans Say Higher Ed Is Headed in the Wrong Direction, But Partisans Disagree on Why* (Washington, DC: Pew Research Center, July 26, 2018), www.pewresearch.org/fact-tank/2018/07/26/most-americans-say-higher-ed-is-heading-in-wrong-direction-but-partisans-disagree-on-why/.

8. College Board, *Trends in College Pricing 2018* (New York, NY: College Board, 2018), p. 3, https://trends.collegeboard.org/sites/default/files/2018-trends-in -college-pricing.pdf.

9. Ibid., 13.

10. Bridget Terry Long, *The College Completion Landscape: Trends, Challenges, and Why It Matters* (Washington, DC: Third Way, May 25, 2018), p. 3, www.t hirdway.org/report/the-college-completion-landscape-trends-challenges-and-why-it -matters.

11. Worthy of note: During the Obama administration, Pell Grants were increased by a significant margin (32 percent), which probably helped to boost overall college

enrollments. Still, this increase did not close the increasing gap between what families could pay for college and the cost of college itself. See Eric Bettinger and Betsy Williams, "Federal and State Financial Aid During the Great Recession," in *How the Financial Crisis and Great Recession Affected Higher Education*, eds. Jeffrey R. Brown and Caroline M. Hoxby (Chicago, IL: University of Chicago Press, 2014).

12. Zack Friedman, "Student Loan Debt Statistics in 2018: A $1.5 Trillion Crisis," *Forbes*, June 13, 2018, www.forbes.com/sites/zackfriedman/2018/06/13/student-loan-debt-statistics-2018/#191002b57310.

13. College Board, *Coming to Our Senses: Education and the American Future. Report of the Commission on Access, Admissions, and Success in Higher Education* (New York, NY: College Board, December 2008), p. 5, https://secure-media.coll egeboard.org/digitalServices/pdf/advocacy/admissions21century/coming-to-our-sens es-college-board-2008.pdf.

14. Andrew Del Banco, *College: What It Was, Is, and Should Be* (Princeton, NJ: Princeton University Press, 2012), p. 148.

15. "Backgrounds and Beliefs of College Freshmen," *Chronicle of Higher Education*, May 1, 2017, www.chronicle.com/interactives/freshmen-survey.

16. *Secretary DeVos Releases Statement on President's Task Force on Apprenticeship Expansion* (Washington, DC: US Department of Education, October 2017), www.ed.gov/news/press-releases/secretary-devos-releases-statement-pres idents-task-force-apprenticeship-expansion. See also *Prepared Remarks from Secretary DeVos to the International Congress on Vocational and Professional Training* (Washington, DC: US Department of Education, June 7, 2018), www.e d.gov/news/speeches/prepared-remarks-secretary-devos-international-congress-voca tional-professional-training.

17. Katherine Mangan, "Confused About 'Free College' Proposals? This Primer Can Help," *Chronicle of Higher Education*, March 18, 2019, www.chronicle.com/ar ticle/Confused-About-How-Free/245917.

18. College Board, *Trends in College Pricing* (Washington, DC: College Board, 2018), https://trends.collegeboard.org/college-pricing.

19. See, e.g., Century Foundation, *Bridging the Higher Education Divide: Strengthening Community Colleges and Restoring the American Dream* (New York, NY: Century Foundation Press, 2013), pp. 3–4.

20. Shapiro, "Student Transfer and Mobility," 6–7.

21. Clifford Adelman, *Moving into Town—and Moving on: The Community College in the Lives of Traditional-Age Students* (Washington, DC: US Department of Education, 2005), www2.ed.gov/rschstat/research/pubs/comcollege/movingint otown.pdf.

22. Stephen J. Handel and Ronald W. Williams, *The Promise of the Transfer Pathway: Opportunities and Challenge for Community College Students Seeking the Baccalaureate Degree* (New York, NY: The College Board, 2012).

23. Theo Pippins, Clive R. Belfield, and Thomas Bailey, *Humanities and Liberal Arts Education Across America's Colleges: How Much Is There?* (New York, NY: Community College Research Center, Teachers College, Columbia University, June 2019), www.ccrc.tc.columbia.edu.

24. US Government Accountability Office, *Higher Education*, 15, www.gao.gov/assets/690/686530.pdf.

25. Rosenbaum, Ahearn, and Rosenbaum, *Bridging the Gaps*.

26. "Tracking" is the pejorative and catch-all word invoking the idea that low-income students and students from underrepresented groups were regularly "tracked" into vocational programs while better-resourced students were encouraged to transfer to a four-year institution to earn a baccalaureate degree. For an extended discussion of this topic, see S. J. Handel, *Recurring Trends and Persistent Themes: A Brief History of Transfer* (New York, NY: College Board, 2013).

27. Goldie Blumenstyk, *American Higher Education in Crisis? What Everyone Needs to Know* (Oxford: Oxford University Press, 2015), p. 142.

28. See David Baker, *The Schooled Society: The Educational Transformation of Global Culture* (Stanford, CA: Stanford University Press, 2014), and Walter W. McMahon, *Higher Learning, Greater Good: The Private and Social Benefits of Higher Education*, Rev. edition (Baltimore, MD: Johns Hopkins University Press, 2017). Both authors make passionate yet empirically rigorous claims on the primacy of higher education as central to the economic advancement of the nation and as an important investment on the part of governments and families in the economic, social, and cultural well-being of individuals.

29. Baker, *The Schooled Society*, 126.

30. Joseph E. Aoun, *Robot-Proof: Higher Education in the Age of Artificial Intelligence* (Cambridge, MA: MIT Press, 2017), p. 67.

31. Ibid., 113.

32. Anthony P. Carnevale, "Confessions of an Education Fundamentalist: Why Grade 12 Is Not the Right End Point for Anyone," in *Minding the Gap: Why Integrating High School with College Makes Sense and How to Do It*, eds. N. Hoffman, J. Vargas, A. Venezia, and M. S. Miller (Cambridge, MA: Harvard University Press, 2007), p. 28.

33. McMahon, *Higher Learning, Greater Good*, 330.

CHAPTER 9

1. Quoted in Goldie Blumenstyk, "Re:Learning," *Chronicle of Higher Education*, December 18, 2019.

2. Paul Fain, "Arizona State Spin-Off Aimed at Corporate Education," *Inside Higher Ed*, March 20, 2019, www.insidehighered.com/quicktakes/2019/03/20/arizona-state-spin-aimed-corporate-education.

3. Goldie Blumenstyk, "How a BYU Campus Is Reshaping Online Education—and the Mormon Faith," *Chronicle of Higher Education*, July 13, 2017, www.chronicle.com/article/How-a-BYU-Campus-Is-Reshaping/240649.

4. *BYU Pathway Connect, Winter 2018 Fact Sheet*, https://pathwaynewsroom.org/facts-and-stats-old/facts-archive/.

5. Blumenstyk, "How a BYU Campus Is Reshaping Online Education."

6. Information about peer-led team learning, as well as useful and comprehensive resources about this educational model and approach, can be found on the International Society's website, https://pltlis.org/vision-mission-goals/.

7. *PathwayConnect Website*, https://byupathway.lds.org/pathwayconnect.

8. Blumenstyk, "How a BYU Campus Is Reshaping Online Education."

9. Blumenstyk, "Re:Learning."

10. Ibid.

11. Quoted in Ibid.

12. Anya Kamenetz, "A New Kind of College Wins Approval in Rhode Island," *National Public Radio*, May 27, 2015, www.npr.org/sections/ed/2015/05/27/40879 3531/a-new-kind-of-college-wins-state-approval-in-rhode-island.

13. "Earn Degrees," *Providence Journal*, November 9, 2018, www.providencej ournal.com/entertainmentlife/20181109/providence-based-college-unbound-helps -minority-low-income-students-earn-degrees.

14. Ibid.

15. Lauren Roy, Liya Escalera, Stephanie Fernandez, Ebru Korbek-Erdogmus, Jennifer Reid, Adam Bush, and John Saltmarsh, "Designing a High-Impact College for Returning Adult Students," *Diversity and Democracy: Building Institutional Capacity for Student Success* 20, no. 4 (Fall 2017), www.aacu.org/diversitydemocrac y/2017/fall/roy.

16. Hummel, "Providence-Based College."

17. Sara Goldrick-Rab, Christine Baker-Smith, Vanessa Coca, Elizabeth Looker, and Tiffani Williams, *College and University Basic Needs Insecurity: A National #RealCollege Survey Report* (The Hope Center for College, Community, and Justice, April 2019), https://hope4college.com/wp-content/uploads/2019/04/HOPE_realcoll ege_National_report_digital.pdf.

18. Louis Soares and Vickie Choitz, *A College Unbound: Lessons on Innovation from a Student-Driven College's Journey Through Regional Accreditation* (Washington, DC: American Council on Education, 2019), www.acenet.edu/Docum ents/A-College-Unbound-Lessons-on-Innovation.pdf#search=college%20unbound.

19. College Unbound, *Guiding Principles*, www.collegeunbound.org/apps/pages/ mission.

20. Jacqueline Thomsen, "A New College for Old Credits," *Inside Higher Ed*, May 26, 2015, www.insidehighered.com/news/2015/05/26/rhode-island-approves -new-college-help-adults-finish-degrees.

21. Diana Strumbos, Donna Linderman, and Carson C. Hicks, "Postsecondary Pathways Out of Poverty: City University of New York Accelerated Study in Associate Programs and the Case for National Policy," *RSF: The Russell Sage Foundation Journal of the Social Sciences* 4, no. 3, Anti-Poverty Policy Initiatives for the United States (February 2018): 100–17, www.jstor.org/stable/10.7758/rsf.20 18.4.3.06.

22. Diana Strumbos and Zineta Kolenovic, "ASAP Graduation Rates by Race/ Ethnicity, Gender and Pell Status," *ASAP Evaluation Brief* (New York, NY: City University of New York, 2016).

23. Strumbos, Linderman, and Hicks, "Postsecondary Pathways Out of Poverty."

24. Strumbos and Kolenovic, "ASAP Graduation Rates."

25. "New Study Shows CUNY's ASAP Program Nearly Doubles Three-Year Graduation Rate of Community College Students Who Need Remedial Education: Cost-per-Degree Is Lower with ASAP," *Press Release* (New York, NY: MDRC, 2015), www.mdrc.org/news/press-release/new-study-shows-cuny-s-asap-program-ne arly-doubles-three-year-graduation-rate.

26. Susan Scrivener, Michael J. Weiss, Alyssa Ratledge, Timothy Rudd, Colleen Sommo, and Hannah Fresques, *Doubling Graduation Rates: Three-Year Effects of CUNY's Accelerated Study in Associate Programs (ASAP) for Developmental Education Students* (New York, NY: MDRC, 2015), p. ES-2.

27. Henry M. Levin and Emma García, *Cost-Effectiveness of Accelerated Study in Associate Programs (ASAP) of the City University of New York (CUNY)* (New York, NY: Center for Benefit-Cost Studies of Education, Teachers College, Columbia University, 2012), p. 19.

28. Henry M. Levin and Emma García, "Accelerating Community College Graduation Rates: A Benefit-Cost Analysis," *Journal of Higher Education* 89, no. 1 (2018): 1–27.

29. Strumbos, Linderman, and Hicks, "Postsecondary Pathways Out of Poverty," 106.

30. Colleen Sommo, Dan Cullinan, and Michelle Manno, with Sean Blake and Erick Alonzo, *Doubling Graduation Rates in a New State: Two-Year Findings from the ASAP Ohio Demonstration* (New York, NY: MDRC, December 2018), p. 1, www .mdrc.org/sites/default/files/ASAP_brief_2018_Final.pdf.

31. Ibid., 9.

32. *CUNY Single Stop Website*, www2.cuny.edu/current-students/student-affairs/ special-programs/single-stop/.

33. Eleanor Eckerson, Lauren Talbourdet, Lindsey Reichlin, Mary Sykes, Elizabeth Noll, and Barbara Gault, "Child Care for Parents in College: A State-by-State Assessment," *Briefing Paper, Institute for Women's Policy Research*, September 2016, www.chronicle.com/blogs/ticker/files/2016/09/Child-Care.pdf.

34. Ibid.

35. Elizabeth Noll, Lindsey Reichlin, and Barbara Gault, "College Students with Children: National and Regional Profiles," *Report, Institute for Women's Policy Research*, January 2017, https://iwpr.org/wp-content/uploads/2017/02/C451-5.pdf.

36. Barbara Gault, Lindsey Reichlin Cruse, Elizabeth Reynolds, and Meghan Froeher, "4.8 Million College Students Are Raising Children," *Fact Sheet, Institute for Women's Policy Research*, November 2014, https://iwpr.org/wp-content/uploads/ wpallimport/files/iwpr-export/publications/C424_Student%20Parents_final.pdf.

37. Ibid.

38. Adolfo Guzman-Lopez, "Nearly 1 in 3 Community College Students Is a Parent: Here's How to Keep Them in Class," *LAist*, March 29, 2019, https://laist.c om/2019/03/29/many_students_cant_balance_being_a_parent_and_going_to_colleg e_--_this_is_how_one_center_helps.php.

39. Barbara Gault, Lindsey Reichlin, and Stephanie Román, "College Affordability for Low-Income Adults: Improving Returns on Investment for Families and Society," *Report, Institute for Women's Policy Research*, April 2014, https://vtechworks.lib.vt.edu/bitstream/handle/10919/87046/LowIncomeAdults.pdf.

40. Gault et al., "4.8 Million College Students Are Raising Children."

41. Barbara Gault, Jessica Milli, and Lindsey Reichlin Cruse, "Investing in Single Mothers' Higher Education: Costs and Benefits to Individuals, Families, and Society," *Institute for Women's Policy Research*, June 2018, https://iwpr.org/wp-content/uploads/2018/06/C469_Single-Mothers-Exec-Summary.pdf.

42. Christopher Booker (Producer), "Little Support in U.S. for College Students Raising Children," *PBS NewsHour* [television broadcast], May 19, 2019, www.pbs.org/newshour/show/little-support-in-us-for-college-students-raising-children.

43. Ibid.

44. *Family Resource Center Website*, http://lavcfamilyresourcecenter.org/enroll/.

45. Booker, "Little Support in U.S. for College Students Raising Children."

46. Cruse was interviewed in Ibid.

47. Noll, Reichlin, and Gault, "College Students with Children."

48. Booker, "Little Support in U.S. for College Students Raising Children."

CHAPTER 10

1. David P. Baker, *The Schooled Society: The Educational Transformation of Global Culture* (Stanford, CA: Stanford University Press, 2014), p. 290.

2. "Indicators of Higher Education Equity in the United States," *2018 Historical Trend Report, Pell Institute for the Study of Opportunity in Higher Education*, http://pellinstitute.org/downloads/publications-Indicators_of_Higher_Education_Equity_in_the_US_2018_Historical_Trend_Report.pdf.

3. Mettler, *From Soldiers to Citizens*, 171–72.

4. "'Food Security' Bill Signed by Gov. Newsom," *Daily Democrat*, July 31, 2019, www.dailydemocrat.com/2019/07/31/food-security-bill-signed-by-gov-newsom/.

Index

PLA. *See* prior-learning assessments (PLA)
Placement Incentive Program, 47
PLA with a Purpose: Prior Learning Assessment & Ohio's College Completion Agenda, 66, 67
policymakers, 12, 16, 23, 46, 119, 121
political populism, 7
populism, 9–11
portfolio-assessment method, 61
portfolio evaluation: and ACE-evaluated workplace training and development, 61; of prior learning, 67
post–Great Recession landscape, 99, 100
postsecondary education, x, 2, 13, 19, 34, 128; lifelong learning survival for, 133–34
postsecondary-education institutions, 57
postsecondary-education landscape, 92
Postsecondary Enrollment Options Act (1985), 51
Present Status of Junior College Terminal Education (Eells), 8
Princeton University, 10, 21, 93
prior-learning assessments (PLA), xii, 58, 59, 87, 89, 109, 110, 126; acceptance and utilization of, 67; avenues for, 61; CBE and, 70; complex juncture of, 64; embrace of, 117; implementation and acceptance of, 127; origins of, 127; positive outcomes for, 60; research, 74; resistance to workplace, 63; transparent and consistent system, 62; usage of, 105
prior-learning credit, 58–60, 64, 71
private colleges, 14, 86, 93
proprietary institutions, 61, 66
public colleges, 14, 86, 93
public-funding, 94

research institutions, 14, 25, 140n22
resources, 12–15
revenues, 12–15
Richardson, Richard C., Jr., 4

Robot-Proof: Higher Education in the Age of Artificial Intelligence (Aoun), 103
Roosevelt, Marni, 115
Rosen, Andrew S., 14
Rosenbaum, James, 30, 101

second chances: celebration of, 34–38; unexamined and unacknowledged, 36–38
Section 127 funding model, 84–85
self-paced course, 61
self-selection bias, 60
single cross-trained advisor, 109, 110
single parenthood, 114
Single Stop College Initiative (CUNY), 113–17, 131
skepticism, 61, 63–64, 128
Slaton, Amy, 74
SNHU. *See* Southern New Hampshire University (SNHU)
social justice issue, 64
"Soldiers to Citizens: The G.I. Bill and the Making of the Greatest Generation" (Mettler), xi
Southern New Hampshire University (SNHU), 83
Speroni, Cecilia, 52, 53
Stanford University, 21, 39, 43
Starbucks, xi, 84, 89, 102, 106, 134
State System PLA Adoption project, 62
statewide systems, 62, 66
Strumbos, Diana, 112
student-centric approach, 109, 113
students: achievement, 37; attracted by educational access, 79; communicate to high school, 43; effort of, 40; at for-profit institutions, 86; internships, 58; lower-income, 72; mobility, 138n4; neo-traditional, 63, 64, 68, 79, 80, 84–85, 106, 115–17, 121. *See also* neo-traditional student; "nontraditional"/"post-traditional-aged," 63; from racial and ethnic backgrounds, 42; regular assessment of, 44; standards-less accommodation

About the Authors

Dr. Eileen Strempel currently serves as the Inaugural Dean of UCLA's Herb Alpert School of Music. Strempel relishes the joy of founding a "start-up company," as the school is the first and only school of music in the University of California (UC) system, and recently formed as a result of a generous $30 million donation by trumpeter, producer, and artist Herb Alpert. As a trained opera singer and a Presidential Scholar in the Arts, Strempel is also a nationally recognized champion for transfer students, and views superb public education as one of the principal social justice issues of our time.

Dean Strempel's scholarly interests focus on the music of women composers, and her work includes numerous recordings, commissions, articles, and edited volumes that examine the political, social, and musical contexts of the most influential female composers of our time. Additional articles and essays include *Transfer Matters More Than Ever, Strategic Collaboration in an Increasingly Interconnected World*, and *Fostering a Receptive Transfer Student Institutional Ecosystem.*

With Stephen J. Handel, the coauthors have completed two previous books, including *Transition and Transformation: Fostering Transfer Student Success* and the follow-up, *Transition and Transformation: New Research Fostering Transfer Student Success,* both with the University of North Georgia Press. Both are proud long-term members of the National Advisory Board for the National Institute for the Study of Transfer Students (NISTS).

Previously, Strempel was the Senior Vice Provost for Academic Affairs at the University of Cincinnati and Professor of Voice at The College-Conservatory of Music (CCM). Prior to that, she served in a variety of roles at Syracuse University over a seventeen-year span, where she was awarded a Kauffman Foundation eProfessorship and the prestigious ACE Fellowship, which she served at Colgate University. Strempel received her Bachelor of

Music degree from the University of Rochester's Eastman School of Music and she received her doctorate from Indiana University's Jacobs School of Music.

Dr. Stephen J. Handel is the Executive Director of Strategic Higher Education Assessment Use and Opportunity at the College Board. In this capacity, he consults with college and university enrollment leaders in the application of fair and effective higher education admission assessments and other resources that benefit students seeking success in postsecondary education. Also at the College Board, Steve served as the inaugural director of the National Office of Community College Initiatives, advancing policies and programs that served the needs of transfer students throughout the United States.

Prior to his position, Steve served as the Associate Vice President—Undergraduate Admissions for the UC system. In this capacity, Handel served as the chief admission officer for the system, providing leadership on freshman and community college transfer policy and practice for the nine UC undergraduate campuses. With over twenty-three years of service at the University of California, Steve served in a variety of leadership roles in such areas as undergraduate admissions, enrollment management, outreach, and student services.

Handel is the author of books and monographs on higher education, including the two-volume series, *Transition and Transformation* (with Eileen Strempel, 2016, 2018) *The Promise of the Transfer Pathway: Opportunity and Challenge for Community College Students Seeking the Baccalaureate Degree* (with Ronald Williams, 2012), and the *Community College Sourcebook: Strategies for Advising Transfer Students from Experienced Community College Counselors* (2009). Articles and essays include *Fairness and Fate in Elite College Admissions, Reigniting the Promise of the Transfer Pathway, College Admission: Now and Then Again, Under Match and the Community College Student, Reimagining Remediation* (with Ronald Williams), *Strengthening the Nation by Narrowing the Gap* (with James Montoya), and *Second Chance, Not Second Class: A Blueprint for Community College Transfer.*

Handel earned his PhD and MA degrees from the University of California, Los Angeles, a BA from California State University, Sacramento, and an AA from Cosumnes River Community College (Sacramento, CA).